The Elements of Education for Curriculum Designers

How should curriculum designers translate abstract learning outcomes into engaging learning experiences that get results? What is the right balance between depth and breadth or between content and skills? What methods should be used to continuously improve a curriculum over time? To answer these kinds of questions, the authors combined research from cutting-edge fields with their own first-hand experience to carefully curate fifty essential elements that demystify the work of curriculum design.

Written for utility, clarity, and practical value, this book provides indispensable professional development for educators working in a wide range of fields—from teachers and school leaders to educational publishers and instructional designers. The elements included are applicable across primary, secondary, and higher education as well as for workforce development programs. *The Elements of Education for Curriculum Designers* is an invaluable resource for anyone aiming to help others learn more effectively.

Rebecca Strauss is the Director of Curriculum Design on the "Tiger Works" Research and Development team at Avenues The World School. She also teaches program development at Columbia University's Teachers College. An experienced learning designer who has led the vision, strategy, development, and implementation of a wide range of education programs for learners of all ages and backgrounds, she holds a B.A. from Barnard College, Columbia University and a Ph.D. from the University of Virginia.

Austin Volz is the Director of Advanced Program Design on the "Tiger Works" Research and Development team at Avenues The World School. He is the lead author of *The Elements of Education for Teachers*. The recipient of both a Fulbright scholarship and Foreign Language and Area Studies Fellowship, Austin holds a B.A. from St. John's College and an Ed.M. from the Harvard Graduate School of Education.

William Lidwell is the Chief Research and Development Officer of the "Tiger Works" Research and Development team at Avenues The World School. He is the author of several books, including the best-selling *Universal Principles of Design*.

T0383601

Also Available from
Routledge Eye On Education
(www.routledge.com/k-12)

The Elements of Education for Teachers:
50 Research-Based Principles Every Educator Should Know
Austin Volz, Julia Higdon, and William Lidwell

What Great Teachers Do Differently, 3e:
Nineteen Things That Matter Most
Todd Whitaker

What Great Principals Do Differently, 3e:
Twenty Things That Matter Most
Todd Whitaker

Mathematizing Your School:
Creating a Culture for Math Success
Nicki Newton and Janet Nuzzie

Coaching to Empower Teachers:
A Framework for Improving Instruction and Well-Being
Catherine Pendleton Hart and Fredrica M. Nash

Better Questioning for Better Learning:
Strategies for Engaged Thinking
Benjamin Stewart Johnson

The Elements of Education for Curriculum Designers

50 Research-Based Principles Every Educator Should Know

Rebecca Strauss, Austin Volz, and William Lidwell

Routledge
Taylor & Francis Group

NEW YORK AND LONDON

First published 2023
by Routledge
605 Third Avenue, New York, NY 10158

and by Routledge
4 Park Square, Milton Park, Abingdon, Oxon, OX14 4RN

Routledge is an imprint of the Taylor & Francis Group, an informa business

Library of Congress Cataloging-in-Publication Data
Names: Strauss, Rebecca (Learning designer), author. | Volz, Austin,
    author. | Lidwell, William, author.
Title: The elements of education for curriculum designers:
    50 research-based principles every educator should know/
    Rebecca Strauss, Austin Volz, and William Lidwelll.
Description: First Edition. | New York: Routledge, 2023.
Identifiers: LCCN 2022029211 | ISBN 9780367336950 (Hardback) |
    ISBN 9780367336943 (Paperback) | ISBN 9780429321283 (eBook)
Subjects: LCSH: Curriculum planning. | Instructional systems—Design. |
    Learning.
Classification: LCC LB2806.15. S768 2023 |
    DDC 375/.001—dc23/eng/20220718
LC record available at https://lccn.loc.gov/2022029211

ISBN: 978-0-367-33695-0 (hbk)
ISBN: 978-0-367-33694-3 (pbk)
ISBN: 978-0-429-32128-3 (ebk)

DOI: 10.4324/9780429321283

Typeset in Palatino
by Apex CoVantage, LLC

Richard and Lois Strauss
Connie Chen

Contents

Acknowledgments

The authors would like to thank many people who have made this work possible.

Dan Veraldi: for every dog walk conversation, happy hour chat, and cooking-turned-writing session that became a chapter. Richard and Lois Strauss: for making it undeniable that the best educators aren't always teachers.

Connie Chen: for the permission to work late as well as the inspiration to laugh and live. Bill and Tamara Volz: for always providing a foundation when everything else is in flux.

We are grateful to our incredible colleagues at Avenues: The World School, who provided us with both direct and indirect support that helped bring this book into existence. Thank you especially to Julia Chun, Amy Rosenberg, Rosanna Satterfield, Jill Butler, Julia Higdon, Jeff Clark, and all the members of the R&D team. Our immense appreciation goes to Luna Zhang, who iterated, adapted, and persevered to create images that complemented our written words.

Finally, we would like to thank everyone at Routledge—and particularly our editor, Lauren Davis—for their patience, professionalism, and support of this book.

Introduction

If you asked a dozen educators how they understand curriculum design, you'd likely hear a dozen different responses:

◆ A superintendent might describe a set of learning standards that articulate what all students should know or be able to do at a given point their learning.

◆ A principal might describe the foundational pillars of their school's academic program.

◆ A teacher might describe how they go about constructing a syllabus or a lesson plan.

◆ A college or guidance counselor might describe their school's diploma requirements.

◆ A provost or dean might describe their university's academic footprint, the range of majors and minors offered, and key areas of the faculty's expertise.

◆ An educational publisher might describe research, trials, peer review, or editorial processes.

◆ A textbook author might describe how they organize content or what gets included in a given chapter and why.

◆ A museum educator might describe resources created for classroom teachers or audio guides developed for school visits.

◆ An edtech provider might describe integrated engagement tools, interoperability, or embedded assessments.

◆ An instructional designer or curriculum writer might describe how they translate learning objectives into activities, resources, and assessments.

◆ A policy analyst might describe concrete data points derived from standardized test results.

◆ A workforce learning and development specialist might describe reskilling initiatives or leadership training programs.

The sheer breadth of these possible understandings of curriculum design is dizzying, made all the more so given that each one is valid and important—and this list is hardly exhaustive. To make matters even trickier, we haven't even begun to touch on how essential stakeholders, such as students and families, might understand curriculum design!

This volume attempts to bridge such disparate understandings of curriculum design by zeroing in on fifty essential elements. These elements were selected using a few key criteria. Each one is informed by classic seminal research that finds new salience when situated the context of cutting-edge fields including cognitive science, educational psychology, and instructional design, as well as by our own first-hand experiences. Each one prioritizes utility, applicability, and practical value. Each one is relevant across the widest possible range of educational contexts, from K-12 schools to higher education and from publishing to edtech. And each one is critical to the difficult work of crafting effective learning experiences for students of all ages and backgrounds.

Because this book is itself a learning experience for readers, we have tried to practice what we preach. As in a well-designed curriculum, we have used a consistent structure for each section, arranged them alphabetically for ease of reference, and embraced brevity and plain-spokenness in our style. Each element has a consistent two-page structure. The left-hand page provides a concise definition, an overview of the research, an explanation of why the principle matters, and a description of how it works. These paragraphs are followed by a "see also" section of related elements. The right-hand page presents guidelines in the form of "Dos" and "Don'ts" for how to apply the principle in practice. These guidelines are not absolute: context, logistical constraints, priorities, and other factors may influence the best method of application. Each element concludes with a quote to inspire further reflection.

These fifty elements are by no means exhaustive. Indeed, it is our hope that this book will inspire further investigation and spark further debate about the essential elements of curriculum design. Because one thing is for sure: in a world characterized by unprecedented complexity and accelerating change, the work of designing effective learning experiences has never been more urgent.

Rebecca Strauss
Austin Volz
William Lidwell

1 Advance Organizers

Introductory devices used to facilitate learning, promote transfer, and enhance recall by contextualizing new information in terms of what learners already know.

Advance organizers help learners understand new information in terms of what they already know. Presented in written, spoken, or visual form prior to the introduction of new material, advance organizers are typically big picture chunks of information. They are distinct from overviews, outlines, inventories, surveys, and synopses in that they are intended to situate (rather than summarize) new material. Examples of advance organizers include concept maps, cause-and-effect diagrams, Venn diagrams, anticipation guides, know, want, learn charts, and storyboards. There are two basic types of advance organizers: expository and comparative.

Expository advance organizers are most useful when the audience has little to no prior knowledge about what is being taught. By spotlighting the key elements of a given unfamiliar topic, expository advance organizers flag what is most important by contextualizing information. For example, before presenting information on how to draw a two-point perspective landscape to an audience with no background in art, an expository advance organizer would first describe horizon lines and vanishing points.

Comparative advance organizers are most useful when the audience already has some prior knowledge about what is being taught. By relating what is about to be learned to what is already known, comparative advance organizers provide a roadmap for how to deepen understanding of a given topic. For example, in teaching more experienced artists about how to draw a two-point perspective landscape, a comparative advance organizer would contrast methods for drawing one-point perspective landscapes to methods for drawing two-point perspective landscapes.

Advance organizers build conceptual understanding, encourage transfer, and promote recall. This is all the more the case when the structure of the advance organizer differs from that of the instruction itself, allowing for dual coding and the presentation of information in multiple formats. For this reason, auditory, graphical, and illustrated advance organizers are often more effective than those that use text alone. Whether the advance organizer is expository or comparative, the technique's effectiveness always hinges upon a well-defined point of entry. Advance organizers are most useful in learning situations where content is presented in a linear fashion, serving as an orienting device to help students situate themselves.

See also Background Knowledge, Five Hat Racks, Framing, Propositional Density, Spiral Curriculum

---

Gurlitt, Johannes, Dummel, Sebastian, Schuster, Silvia, and Nückles, Matthias. 2012. "Differently Structured Advance Organizers Lead to Different Initial Schemata and Learning Outcomes." *Instructional Science* 40 (2): 351–369.

Mayer, Richard E. 1979. "Twenty Years of Research on Advance Organizers: Assimilation Theory is Still the Best Predictor of Results." *Instructional Science* 8 (2): 133–167.

DOI: 10.4324/9780429321283-1

DO ···

- ◆ Do use advance organizers to contextualize new information.
- ◆ Do use expository advance organizers when learners have little to no background knowledge about the topic being introduced.
- ◆ Do use comparative advance organizers when learners already have some background knowledge about the topic being introduced.
- ◆ Do only use advance organizers at the beginning of instructional units.

 **DON'T** ···

- ◆ Don't use expository advance organizers for material that is tangential or digressive.
- ◆ Don't use comparative advance organizers for material that is superficial or inconsequential.
- ◆ Don't use advance organizers to summarize information at the end of a unit.

 REFLECT ···

Researchers have demonstrated improvements in students' comprehension and recall from advance organizers that rely on familiar structures when they are presented in writing, orally, or pictorially. These studies indicate that when students are provided with an organizational structure in which to fit new knowledge, they learn more effectively and efficiently than when they are left to deduce this conceptual structure for themselves.

Ambrose, Susan A., Bridges, Michael W., DiPietro, Michele, Lovett, Marsha C., and Norman, Marie K. 2010. *How Learning Works: Seven Research-based Principles for Smart Teaching.* John Wiley & Sons.

2 Aesthetics

Techniques of visual and writing style used to increase the appeal and effectiveness of a curriculum.

Aesthetic curricula are characterized by clear, straightforward writing and visual aids that are both elegant and integral to the design. They are generally perceived more positively than jargon-heavy curricula or curricula that are overloaded with unnecessary or distracting graphics. As a result, aesthetic curricula have a higher probability of being adopted and are more likely to generate higher levels of investment and attachment from key stakeholders including teachers, students, school administrators, and district leaders. As such, they achieve better learning at scale.

This element applies at all levels of curriculum design, from high-level learning outcomes to daily lessons. For example, consider the following learning outcome from Common Core's Grade 2 Mathematics standards: "draw a picture graph and a bar graph (with single-unit scale) to represent a data set with up to four categories. Solve simple put-together, take-apart, and compare problems using information presented in a bar graph." This standard is riddled with unaesthetic complexity: the two sentences represent two different outcomes; the use of jargon (such as "put-together, take-apart, and compare problems") makes the language difficult to parse; and without a visual aid representing what a successful picture graph or bar graph would look like, the outcome is difficult to assess. To make this standard more aesthetic, it could be rephrased more plainly as "record and interpret data presented in the following graphical forms" and be accompanied by labeled visual examples of each graphical form.

Resources for individual lessons should employ the same aesthetic principles. The goals of a given handout or worksheet should be clearly stated. Instructions should be phrased simply, briefly, and without the use of jargon. Thoughtful decisions should be made with regard to all visual components including font choice, the use of clip art or other graphic elements, and document layout.

Because aesthetics play a key role in how curricula are used and implemented, teachers and students are less likely to perceive shortcomings in a well-written and visually evocative curriculum. A textbook that is overly pedantic in its writing style, that is printed in a dated font such as Comic Sans, or that utilizes stock images invites a heavy-handed critique from its users. By contrast, a textbook that is written in clear and accessible language, printed in a readable modern font, and incorporates dynamic and original graphics demonstrates a level of intention and care that users perceive more favorably. Even if the unaesthetic textbook actually has higher quality content, it risks lower acceptance and inferior implementation due to a lack of aesthetics. Likewise, even if the more aesthetic textbook has lower quality content, its aesthetic superiority would make teachers and students less likely to notice and more likely to be tolerant of its shortcomings.

See also Framing, Labeling Systems, Student-Facing vs. Teacher-Facing, Textbooks, Scalability

Kurosu, Masaaki, and Kashimura, Kaori. 1995. "Apparent Usability vs. Inherent Usability: Experimental Analysis on the Determinants of the Apparent Usability." In *Conference Companion on Human Factors in Computing Systems*, 292–293. ACM Association for Computing Machinery.

DOI: 10.4324/9780429321283-2

✓ DO ···

- ◆ Do use a writing style that is clear, accessible, succinct, and jargon-free.
- ◆ Do incorporate visual aids that provide complementary understanding to the text.
- ◆ Do recognize teachers' and learners' limited willingness to parse, navigate, and use an unaesthetic curriculum.
- ◆ Do err on the side of less is more aesthetic.

✗ DON'T ···

- ◆ Don't use a writing style that is vague, dense, verbose, or jargon-heavy.
- ◆ Don't incorporate inessential or superfluous resources.
- ◆ Don't underestimate the role of aesthetics in how a curriculum is perceived.

❝ REFLECT ···

For designers, the visceral response is about immediate perception: the pleasantness of a mellow, harmonious sound or the jarring, irritating scratch of fingernails on a rough surface. Here is where the style matters: appearances, whether sound or sight, touch or smell, drive the visceral response. This has nothing to do with how usable, effective, or understandable the product is. It is all about attraction or repulsion. Great designers use their aesthetic sensibilities to drive these visceral responses.

Norman, Don. 2013. *The Design of Everyday Things: Revised and Expanded Edition*. Basic Books.

3 Alignment

The intentional continuity, consistency, and connectivity of a curriculum both within and across areas of study.

A curriculum is vertically aligned when a given content area is intentionally coordinated over time—as, for example, when eighth-grade history purposefully builds off of seventh-grade history. A curriculum is horizontally aligned when multiple content areas are intentionally coordinated within a given time frame—as, for example, when eighth-grade history is in purposeful dialogue with eighth-grade science. Vertical alignment ensures that the curriculum is free of gaps and redundancies. Horizontal alignment produces a better integrated learning experience with greater opportunities for transfer. Both vertically and horizontally aligned curricula are characterized by continuity, consistency, and connectivity.

Continuity refers to the intentional repetition of key knowledge and skills across a curriculum. For example, in a vertically aligned curriculum that is continuous, probability claims might be introduced early in the math curriculum and returned to repeatedly at well-chosen intervals. In a horizontally aligned curriculum that is continuous, evaluating probability claims can extend beyond the math curriculum and into the literacy curriculum when students make predictions about and weigh the likelihood of what will happen next in the plot of a story. This increases both the depth and breadth of the curriculum as a whole.

Consistency refers to the use of common elements, constructions, and styles across a curriculum. For example, in a vertically aligned curriculum that is consistent, a common definition of what constitutes a strong thesis statement is shared across English courses at all grade levels. In a horizontally aligned curriculum that is consistent, that same definition is shared not only within all English courses, but also across history, science, math, and so on. This reduces the cognitive overhead required to navigate aspects of the curriculum that are not directly related to learning outcomes (such as understanding each teacher's idiosyncratic definition of what makes a thesis statement strong) and redirects those cognitive resources to the more salient aspects of the task (such as composing strong thesis statements).

Connectivity refers to how knowledge is bridged across different parts of a curriculum. For example: in a vertically aligned curriculum that is connective, students might demonstrate near transfer by learning about cell specialization and then connecting that knowledge to evaluating a particular stem cell treatment. In a horizontally aligned curriculum that is connective, students might demonstrate far transfer by learning about cell specialization and then connecting that knowledge to interpreting how complexity evolves from simplicity in a work of literature. In this regard, connectivity is the consummation of vertical and horizontal alignment: it makes possible a more unified curriculum and, in turn, a more unified learning experience.

See also Breadth vs. Depth, Curriculum Maps, Interdisciplinarity, Learning Progressions, Spiral Curriculum, Usability vs. Learnability

---

Tyler, Ralph. 1949. *Basic Principles of Curriculum and Instruction*. The University of Chicago Press.

DOI: 10.4324/9780429321283-3

✓ DO

- ◆ Do avoid gaps and redundancies by mapping a content area over the whole arc of the curriculum.
- ◆ Do integrate learning experiences and facilitate transfer by coordinating across multiple content areas within a given time frame.
- ◆ Do use spiraling, parallel construction, and bridging techniques both within and across content areas to achieve alignment in a curriculum.

✗ DON'T

- ◆ Don't design or develop courses in a given content area in silos.
- ◆ Don't design or develop courses in a given time frame in silos.
- ◆ Don't underestimate the value of curriculum documentation tools such as crosswalks and curriculum maps in facilitating alignment.

❝ REFLECT

Important changes in human behavior are not produced overnight. No single learning experience has a very profound influence on the learner. Changes in ways of thinking, in fundamental habits, in major operating concepts, in attitudes, in abiding interests and the like, develop slowly. It is only after months and years that we are able to see major educational objectives taking marked concrete shape.

Tyler, Ralph. 1949. *Basic Principles of Curriculum and Instruction.* The University of Chicago Press.

4   Background Knowledge

What learners already know about a given topic at the outset of instruction.

Background knowledge enables learners to connect new information to old and to make sense out of unfamiliar ideas. While many factors—including the teacher's skill, the student's interest, and the content's difficulty—influence how students absorb new information, background knowledge is one of the largest determiners of how well and how quickly learners understand and internalize new knowledge. For example, studies have shown that if strong readers with no background knowledge are given an article about baseball and weak readers with some background knowledge about baseball are given the same article, the latter group will exhibit higher levels of comprehension. This is because background knowledge is more predictive of comprehension than literacy skills. As this example demonstrates, background knowledge is required to anchor and situate skill development.

A strong curriculum design should leverage learners' background knowledge or scaffold it when it does not exist. The most effective strategy for this is a spiral curriculum. A spiral curriculum provides scaffolding that encourages learners to build new mental models and to integrate new information into pre-existing mental models. By creating a multitude of connection points, a spiral curriculum also allows learners to acquire more new knowledge because it can be integrated into mental models more readily. But even with a spiral curriculum, learners' background knowledge on a given topic can still vary widely. Not all background knowledge is acquired through the curriculum: for example, some learners studying astronomy may spend weekends at a planetarium or have telescopes at home, while others may be learning about stars and planets for the first time.

Curriculum designers should first define what the prerequisite background knowledge is for a given unit or course—for example, algebra is a prerequisite for calculus—so as to set learners up for success in connecting the new material to what they already know. While it might be tempting to begin a unit or course with a pre-test designed to assess background knowledge (a technique commonly used in math to gauge optimal placement), these measurement tools should be employed with caution. They are usually cumbersome, ineffective, and often end up creating negative learning experiences for students.

Instead, units and courses should begin with advance organizers, which engage and expand learners' understanding by introducing new information in terms of the prerequisite background knowledge they already have. Expository advance organizers should be used for learners who have little or no prior knowledge of the subject matter (for example, introducing simple variables in pre-algebra), while comparative advance organizers help learners with more background knowledge enrich their understanding of the topic at hand (for example, a Venn diagram comparing linear algebra to multivariable calculus).

See also Advance Organizers, Content vs. Skills, Levels, Learning Progressions, Mental Models, Minimalism, Spiral Curriculum

Marzano, Robert J. 2004. *Building Background Knowledge for Academic Achievement: Research on What Works in Schools*. ASCD.

Recht, Donna R., and Leslie, Lauren. 1988. "Effect of Prior Knowledge on Good and Poor Readers' Memory of Text." *Journal of Educational Psychology* 80 (1): 16.

DOI: 10.4324/9780429321283-4

DO ··

- ◆ Do use advance organizers and a spiral curriculum to help learners connect new information to what they already know and integrate new material into pre-existing mental models.
- ◆ Do identify prerequisite background knowledge and develop strategies to fill gaps for those who need it.
- ◆ Do situate skill development in contexts that connect with learners' background knowledge.

 DON'T ···

- ◆ Don't substitute access to search engines and related resources with the development of background knowledge.
- ◆ Don't assume that learners' background knowledge has been acquired exclusively through the curriculum.
- ◆ Don't use pre-tests to assess background knowledge or determine placement.

 REFLECT ··

In fact, given the relationship between academic background knowledge and academic achievement, one can make the case that it should be at the top of any list of interventions intended to enhance student achievement. If not addressed by schools, academic background can create great advantages for some students and great disadvantages for others.

Marzano, Robert J. 2004. *Building Background Knowledge for Academic Achievement: Research on What Works In Schools*. ASCD.

5 Backward Design

A process by which learning experiences are derived from learning goals and assessment evidence to increase curricular effectiveness.

Consider the following scenario: a curriculum designer building a tenth-grade English course creates the syllabus by selecting favorite texts (for example, *Their Eyes Were Watching God* and *Pride and Prejudice*), develops lessons on salient topics (racial injustice and marriage), chooses instructional methods (close reading and Socratic discussion), and assigns deliverables (an interpretative essay and an adaptation). While this curriculum might well be thought-provoking, engaging, and fun, it is not at all clear what students are meant to know or be able to do as a result of having taken the course. As such, there is no way to assess if students have learned what was intended—which is also to say that there is no way to gauge whether or not the curriculum is effective.

The best designs derive from a clear end goal and curriculum is no exception. In backward design, the desired results of a learning experience are identified first, followed by what will serve as evidence of learning. This brings greater clarity about what is essential (and what is extraneous) to the learning experience and ensures that the activities, lessons, and materials selected are focused, lean, and goal-driven. Further, backward design embeds within the curriculum the means of its own assessment: the effectiveness of the curriculum is determined by whether and how well students have learned what was intended. Data on student performance should be collected, analyzed, and used to continuously improve the curriculum through iteration.

While backward design may seem only common sense, it runs counter to much conventional practice. Too often, curriculum design is approached as a means to cover a given subject area, or as a series of interrelated activities, or even (as in the example above) as a well-intentioned and engaging but ultimately rudderless collection of materials, lessons, topics, pedagogies, and assignments. Further, assessments are frequently cobbled together at the end of a unit, or connected unevenly to the full range of content, or borrowed from a textbook or website. By contrast, in backward design what serves as evidence of learning is identified prior to the creation of the unit itself, resulting in activities and lessons that better set students up for success in the assessment, greater clarity about expectations, and stronger overall student performance. By aligning desired results, key performance indicators, and the learning experiences designed to produce them, backward design ensures a more effective curriculum.

See also Curriculum Assessment, Iteration, Five Hat Racks, Learning Outcomes, Templates

Wiggins, Grant, Wiggins, Grant P., and McTighe, Jay. 2005. *Understanding by Design*. ASCD.

DOI: 10.4324/9780429321283-5

DO ···

- ◆ Do begin designing curricula by naming the desired results of the given learning experience.
- ◆ Do identify what will serve as evidence of learning prior to creating a given unit or course.
- ◆ Do design and curate lessons, activities, and resources to achieve the desired results and set learners up for success.

 **DON'T** ···

- ◆ Don't use favorite texts, topics, pedagogies, or assignments as the starting point for the design of a curriculum.
- ◆ Don't design activities or select resources for a given unit or course before deciding what will serve as evidence of learning.
- ◆ Don't include any extraneous resources, lessons, or activities that do not directly serve the learning goal and position learners for success.

REFLECT ···

Our lessons, units, and courses should be logically inferred from the results sought, not derived from the methods, books, and activities with which we are most comfortable. Curriculum should lay out the most effective ways of achieving specific results . . . in short, the best designs derive backward from the learnings sought.

Wiggins, Grant, and McTighe, Jay. 2005. *Understanding by Design.* ASCD.

6 Breadth vs. Depth

The degree to which a curriculum prioritizes general exposure or concentrated coverage.

The breadth of a curriculum is the span of subjects and topics covered and the depth of a curriculum is the extent of the concentration in a given subject or topic. Striking the right balance between breadth and depth in a curriculum is essential because acquiring broad knowledge is the foundation for developing deep knowledge just as building up depth is the gateway for generalizing to breadth.

A broad curriculum equips students with necessary context to learn new information. This is essential to building background knowledge, which is one of the largest determiners of how well and how quickly learners understand and internalize new knowledge and skills. For example: a broad biology survey lays the foundation for developing familiarity with ecology, genetics, and neuroscience and situates skills like recording observations and testing hypotheses in a rich context. A broad range of learning experiences also empowers students to discover their own talents and passions before specializing; it is for this reason that many schools do not offer elective courses until the last two years of high school.

A deep curriculum equips students with better long-term retention of information because sustained analysis promotes better recall than superficial analysis. For example, a project in which students annotate a poem and contextualize each of its referents improves the likelihood that the poem will be recalled because of the additional thought required to perform the task. By encouraging more extensive and thorough analysis, a deep curriculum provides more opportunities for students to arrive at original insights. Depth in a curriculum also empowers students to develop fluency in highly specialized topics, such as quantum theory, symbolic logic, or the Iranian Revolution. Deep learning experiences that are designed to cultivate expertise in niche areas require time, effort, and concentration to develop and deliver; this is why most colleges and universities employ doctorate-holding faculty to create and teach such courses and why students are required to take many classes in a given subject area in order to earn a major.

Two key interrelated factors should be weighed to determine when to employ a broad curricular approach and when to employ a deep one: the context and complexity of the topic. Context refers to the background knowledge students already have about the topic. Complexity refers to the extent of analysis required to understand the topic. If learners have little context for a topic or if the topic is straightforward and uncomplicated, then a broad approach should be favored. If learners already have contextual information about a topic or if the topic is complex and difficult to understand, then a deep approach should be favored.

See also Background Knowledge, Content vs. Skills, Learning Progressions, Minimalism, Specialization, Threshold Concepts

Hirsch Jr, E. D. 2001. "Seeking Both Breadth and Depth in the Curriculum." *Educational Leadership* 59 (2): 22–25.
Parker, Walter C., Lo, Jane, Yeo, Angeline Jude, Valencia, Sheila W., Nguyen, Diem, Abbott, Robert D., Nolen, Susan B., Bransford, John D., and Vye, Nancy J. 2013. "Beyond Breadth-Speed-Test: Toward Deeper Knowing and Engagement in an Advanced Placement Course." *American Educational Research Journal* 50 (6): 1424–1459.

DOI: 10.4324/9780429321283-6

✅ DO

- Do strike a balance between breadth and depth based on the topic's context and complexity.
- Do favor breadth when the topic is clear-cut and unambiguous.
- Do favor depth when the topic is complicated and nuanced.
- Do use learning goals as the anchor for striking the right balance between breadth and depth.

❌ DON'T

- Don't underestimate or overestimate the background knowledge learners already have about a given topic.
- Don't underestimate or overestimate the amount of analysis students may require to understand a given topic.
- Don't go deeper or broader than needed to achieve the desired results.

❝ REFLECT

[We should . . .] abandon the sloganized polarity between deep understanding and the rote learning of mere facts. We cannot gain deep understanding without having broad factual knowledge. On the other hand, piling up more and more facts that don't really add much to our understanding or ability to learn wastes our time.

Hirsch Jr, E. D. 2001. "Seeking Both Breadth and Depth in the Curriculum." *Educational Leadership* 59 (2): 22–25.

7 Capstones

Culminating, integrative learning experiences that provide opportunities to synthesize ideas and apply previous learning in real-world contexts.

While a capstone is a culminating learning experience, not all culminating learning experiences are capstones. Much more than an exercise in closure, a capstone is designed to promote transfer. To that end, capstones extend beyond one particular subject area and require students to apply broadly portable skills such as critical thinking, problem-solving, communication, research, goal-setting, and planning in real-world contexts.

Because capstones ask students to apply what they have studied in authentic contexts, they result in a final product that has real-world applicability. Examples of capstone products include: exhibiting a portfolio of work in a public space; crafting and pitching a viable business plan; conducting research over an extended period of time and presenting findings in a white paper or oral presentation; designing and building a tool that addresses a particular need; planning and hosting an event, symposium, or conference; and so on. No one capstone product type is inherently better than another. However, the product type should be selected based on its authenticity. The goal is to provide students with an opportunity to apply the knowledge and skills they have developed in a real-world context through creating the capstone product.

Capstones have many benefits. Because learners tend to remember the last thing they did the most vividly, a well-designed capstone promotes retention of the most important ideas. Further, capstones have been shown to increase engagement, improve confidence, enhance college or career readiness, and equip students with demonstrable proficiency. Because they are designed to promote transfer, capstones are inherently interdisciplinary. And because they are designed to provide opportunities for application in authentic contexts, capstones encourage students to connect what they have learned to real communities.

Criticisms of capstones have tended to focus on the quality of execution. Because capstones require a significant investment of time and resources, expectations about their pay-off are understandably high. If a capstone reflects unrigorous academic standards or lacks clear methods for evaluation, students tend to create superficial products that are not of much demonstrable educational value. Further, overwhelming students with multiple capstones in multiple courses simultaneously results in lower-quality products. Curriculum designers should favor a single, interdisciplinary capstone that promotes transfer by asking students to draw meaningful connections across subject areas and demonstrate proficiency through a thoughtfully-created product with real-world applicability.

See also Interdisciplinarity, Learning Progressions, Learning Tasks, Rigor, Threshold Concepts

Great Schools Partnerships. "Capstones Projects." *The Glossary of Educational Reform*. www.edglossary.org/capstone-project/

Schank, Roger C. 1995. *Tell Me A Story: Narrative and Intelligence*. Northwestern University Press.

DOI: 10.4324/9780429321283-7

DO ··

♦ Do use capstones to promote transfer by focusing on critical thinking, problem-solving, communication, research, goal-setting, and planning in real-world contexts.

♦ Do employ rigorous academic standards and clear methods for evaluation in capstone projects.

♦ Do favor single, interdisciplinary capstone projects that ask learners to make meaningful connections across content areas.

♦ Do design capstone projects at the end of an extended sequence of study.

DON'T ···

♦ Don't design culminating learning tasks that are inauthentic or simplistic.

♦ Don't use contrived, corny, or inauthentic contexts for capstones.

♦ Don't assign multiple capstones in multiple courses simultaneously.

REFLECT ···

The peak-end rule is a psychological heuristic in which people judge an experience largely based on how they felt at its peak (i.e., its most intense point) and at its end, rather than based on the total sum or average of every moment of the experience.

Kahneman, D., Fredrickson, B. L., Schreiber, C. A., and Redelmeier, D. A. 1993. "When More Pain Is Preferred to Less: Adding a Better End." *Psychological Science* 4 (6): 401–405.

8   Case Studies

Real-world, problem-based scenarios that encourage students to move from concrete examples to generalizable principles.

Case studies encourage students to understand a specific problem, analyze relevant data, weigh the advantages and limitations of different approaches, draw informed conclusions, and present viable solutions. They also create a bridge between theory and practice by enabling students to arrive at general principles through sustained analysis of a concrete example. Case studies have been shown to increase students' interest, motivation, and engagement and to improve their retention. While they are most frequently used in professional education such as business school, law school, and medical school, case studies are powerful curricular tools for any academic program where the goal is for students to figure out high-level principles for themselves and apply what they have learned to real-world situations.

Case studies help students to develop and hone a wide range of highly transferable skills—such as critical thinking, problem-solving, analysis, team leadership, decision making, coping with ambiguity, and managing competing or even conflicting goals—and to situate those skills in real-world contexts. When a case study approach is used to develop these skills, having students work together as a team increases the overall effectiveness. An interactive approach promotes collaboration, allows students to learn from one another's perspectives and insights, models how to solve a given problem multiple ways, and immerses students in an authentic team-based context.

Case study formats can range from a brief vignette of a simple scenario to a detailed description of a complex situation. Whether to use a simple or a detailed case study depends upon the learning goals, but a few key elements should always characterize the design of the curriculum. Case studies should present a real-world problem. Context for the problem should be provided along with some supporting data. Depending on the level of detail, the data might include key figures and selected quotations or complete spreadsheets and full transcripts of testimony. Discussion prompts and learning tasks such as role-plays, debates, and simulations should support the creation of a recommendation, action plan, or proposal. To ensure that case studies are relevant and authentic, curriculum designers should partner with subject-matter experts to develop scenarios, provide context, curate data, and craft discussion prompts and learning tasks.

See also Background knowledge, framing, Mental Models, Rigor, Propositional density, storytelling, Subject-Matter Experts

---

Andersen, E., and Schiano, B. 2014. *Teaching with Cases: A Practical Guide*. Harvard Business Press Books.
Garvin, D. 2003. "Making the Case: Professional Education for the World of Practice." *Harvard Magazine*, September–October: 56.
Penn, Marion L., Currie, Christine S. M., Hoad, Kathryn A., and O'Brien, Frances A. 2016. "The Use of Case Studies in OR Teaching." *Higher Education Pedagogies* 1 (1): 16–25.

DOI: 10.4324/9780429321283-8

DO ··

- ◆ Do use case studies when the learning goal is for learners to figure out high-level principles for themselves or apply what they have learned to real-world situations.
- ◆ Do design case studies to encourage role-play, discussion, and collaboration.
- ◆ Do partner with subject-matter experts to develop scenarios, provide context, curate data, and craft discussion prompts and learning tasks to ensure authenticity and relevance.
- ◆ Do use case studies to make learning as concrete and as relevant as possible
- ◆ Do use case studies to facilitate transfer.

 DON'T ··

- ◆ Don't present cases that have an exclusive or single solution.
- ◆ Don't present cases without context and supporting data.
- ◆ Don't present farcical or unrealistic scenarios.

REFLECT ··

Cases teach students to size up business problems quickly while considering the broader organizational, industry, and societal context. Students recall concepts better when they are set in a case, much as people remember words better when used in context. Cases teach students how to apply theory in practice and how to induce theory from practice. The case method cultivates the capacity for critical analysis, judgment, decision-making, and action.

Nohria, Nitin. 2021. "What the Case Study Method Really Teaches." *Harvard Business Review*, December 21. https://hbr.org/2021/12/what-the-case-study-method-really-teaches

9 Content vs. Skills

The degree to which a curriculum prioritizes subject-specific knowledge or transferable application.

Content is the span of subjects and topics covered in a curriculum and skills are the means by which that knowledge is applied. Advocates of content-driven curricula stress that facts are essential to all learning, while those in favor of skills-focused approaches argue that learning facts without applying them lacks real-world relevance. Striking the right balance between content and skills in a curriculum is essential: mastering content is the foundation for effective application, just as the ability to apply learning in authentic contexts is the very reason to have learned content in the first place.

In general, content knowledge is a prerequisite to skill development. For example: students must first be able to identify the organisms in an ecosystem and the physical environment with which they interact before predicting the impact of introducing a new species or proposing solutions to address a change in the food web. Because working memory is limited, students looking up new information at the same time as they are trying to use that information to solve a problem are unlikely to be successful at either task. By contrast, when studied over time, new information becomes part of long-term memory. This allows students to build their background knowledge and situate new material, enabling them to apply what has been learned more effectively.

In order to be retained, content must be used. To that end, ample skills-based opportunities to apply understanding of content should be baked into the design of the curriculum. Essential content knowledge—including material that aligns to a school's mission, is relevant for the largest number of students, and is likely to be useful in a wide range of future scenarios—should be prioritized. Extraneous content should be pruned to create space for skills-based learning experiences, which promote long-term retention by encouraging students to apply what they have learned in authentic contexts.

It is worth noting that literacy and foreign language curricula require an especially strong emphasis on content because both involve two layers: decoding and comprehension. Decoding is a focus on understanding the language itself, while comprehension is the ability to understand what the deciphered language means. Achieving comprehension requires students to have content knowledge that they can draw upon and use to make sense out of what they are decoding. For example: it would be much easier for students to sound out and predict the meaning of an unfamiliar word on a Farsi menu if they are familiar with Persian cuisine and eating in restaurants. In this way, comprehension eases working memory limitations. By making the meaning of the writing familiar, students can focus on structure and phonetics. In both literacy and language learning, familiarity with a content area increases overall comprehension.

See also Background Knowledge, Breadth vs. Depth, Learning Objectives, Learning Outcomes

---

Connor, Carol McDonald, Dombek, Jennifer, Crowe, Elizabeth C., Spencer, Mercedes, Tighe, Elizabeth L., Coffinger, Sean, Zargar, Elham, Wood, Taffeta, and Petscher, Yaacov. 2017. "Acquiring Science and Social Studies Knowledge in Kindergarten Through Fourth Grade: Conceptualization, Design, Implementation, and Efficacy Testing of Content-Area Literacy Instruction (CALI)." *Journal of Educational Psychology* 109 (3): 301.
Recht, Donna R., and Leslie, Lauren. 1988. "Effect of Prior Knowledge on Good and Poor Readers' Memory of Text." *Journal of Educational Psychology* 80 (1): 16.

DOI: 10.4324/9780429321283-9

DO ···

- ◆ Do introduce content knowledge before introducing skills that depend on that knowledge
- ◆ Do prioritize content that is the most pertinent for the largest number of learners and is most likely to be useful in the widest range of contexts.
- ◆ Do limit the amount of new content to four to six items at a time.
- ◆ Do provide ample skills-based opportunities for learners to apply their understanding in authentic contexts.
- ◆ Do intentionally alternate between skill-driven and content-driven activities in the learning experience.

 DON'T ···

- ◆ Don't focus on content to the exclusion of skills or on skills to the exclusion of content.
- ◆ Don't design courses that only introduce content without skills-driven activities that facilitate application.
- ◆ Don't overload units or courses with inessential, extraneous, or excessive content.

 REFLECT ···

A reading of the research literature from cognitive science shows that knowledge does much more than just help students hone their thinking skills: It actually makes learning easier. Knowledge is not only cumulative, it grows exponentially. Those with a rich base of factual knowledge find it easier to learn more—the rich get richer . . . So, the more knowledge students accumulate, the smarter they become.

Willingham, Daniel. 2006. "How Knowledge Helps." *American Educator*, Spring.

10 Course Guides

An essential communication tool that orients learners and external audiences in navigating an academic program.

A course guide (also known as a course catalog in higher education) provides a holistic overview of a given program of study including descriptions of academic pillars, summaries of course offerings, and expectations around learning experiences. A strong course guide sets curricular expectations for internal stakeholders including students, faculty, school leaders, and families. It is also essential for external communications, licensing, and accreditation. Course guides can take a wide range of forms, but it is essential that they contain the following components: a clear organizational system, consistent use of that system, and key distinguishing features of the curriculum.

First, an organizational system for the course guide must be selected. There is no one right way to organize a course guide; rather, the system should be selected based on what will be most useful to the largest group of stakeholders seeking to navigate the program. For example: a K-12 school might divide their course guide into lower, middle, and upper school sections; a culinary institute might highlight required foundations of cooking courses before listing electives such as pastry or restaurant management; a small liberal arts college might structure the course guide by academic department; and so on. In this way, the organizational system enables audiences to explore a more tightly defined subset of the curriculum, such as the freshman year experience or the four mother sauces or the set of requirements for an anthropology major.

Once an organization system for the course guide has been established, it should be used consistently. No matter the organization system, information within each section of the course guide should be presented using the same frameworks and labeling systems. For example, it should not be the case that the history department organizes its courses by geographical region, but the science department provides a sequence from kindergarten through graduation. Avoiding such pitfalls will require high levels of alignment and strategic coordination between multiple creators of course guide content.

Finally, a good course guide should highlight distinguishing features of the curriculum such as signature learning experiences, distribution requirements, and interdisciplinary programs. This underscores the intentionally interconnected, mission-driven curricular architecture. It also allows audiences to see the curriculum's bigger picture aims, explore relationships between courses, and become interested in new aspects of the curriculum they might not have discovered otherwise. Because these sections are such powerful tools, they should be used sparingly and strategically: too many will create clutter in the course guide and audiences will grow confused if the importance or mission-alignment is unclear.

See also Alignment, Crosswalks, Curriculum Maps, Five Hat Racks, Labeling Systems

Rosenfeld, Louis, and Morville, Peter. 2002. *Information Architecture for the World Wide Web*. O'Reilly Media, Inc.

DOI: 10.4324/9780429321283-10

DO ···

◆ Do design the course guide with an eye towards both internal and external stakeholders' needs and expectations.

◆ Do select the organizational system for the course guide based on what will be useful for the largest number of stakeholders.

◆ Do use consistent labeling systems and frameworks across different sections of the course guide.

DON'T ···

◆ Don't vary the organizational system, labeling systems, or frameworks for the course guide when describing different divisions or departments.

◆ Don't place key information such as graduation requirements in a difficult to find or obscure section of the course guide.

◆ Don't assume audiences will read the course guide linearly or sequentially.

REFLECT ···

It is impossible to create a perfect organization system . . . However, by recognizing the importance of perspective, by striving to understand the intended audiences through user research and testing, and by providing multiple navigation pathways, you can do a better job of organizing information for public consumption than your coworker does on his desktop computer.

Rosenfeld, Louis, and Morville, Peter. 2002. *Information Architecture for the World Wide Web*. O'Reilly Media, Inc.

11 Crosswalks

A tool used to document, cross-reference, and align curricula in order to inform iteration and guide implementation strategy.

The term "crosswalk" is borrowed from metadata transfer, where it refers to the translation of elements from one schema to another. A curriculum crosswalk serves the same purpose: it maps sets of learning outcomes to one another. A crosswalk is a valuable tool for achieving common curricular goals such as documentation, cross-reference, comparison, alignment, gap analysis, iteration planning, and implementation strategy.

Crosswalks enable educators to identify where two curricula share roughly equivalent outcomes. They also serve as an important gap analysis tool by illuminating where curricula do not align. This information then serves as a strategic roadmap that informs what needs to be adapted or created in order to bring the two curricula into alignment. Any two sets of learning outcomes can be crosswalked in this fashion to compare goals, identify gaps, and devise plans. For example, a crosswalk can be used to inform the design of elective courses that prepare students to take Advanced Placement exams or SAT II subject tests by ensuring alignment to the outcomes that those assessments measure. Crosswalks are also commonly used by U.S. public schools when navigating the adoption of Common Core. By mapping the learning goals of state standards to the national Common Core standards, a curriculum crosswalk documents where the two curricula overlap and where they diverge.

Crosswalk creation should be led by a small working group of curriculum designers rather than a large group of teachers and administrators. The team is responsible for developing, maintaining, reviewing, and updating the crosswalk. All relevant learning goals from the two curricula being cross-referenced should be assembled in a spreadsheet or a document with two columns. Outcomes from one set of standards in the left-hand column should correspond to outcomes from the second set of standards in the right-hand column. If the grain size of the outcomes is not aligned, it may be the case that several outcomes of a smaller grain size from one curriculum must be taken together in order to demonstrate equivalency to a single outcome of a larger grain size from the second curriculum.

Once the two curricula have been organized in cross-reference to one another, the crosswalk can be used to highlight gaps that need filling as well as excesses that need pruning. This informs the strategy for curricular iteration. New assessments should be designed for revised or new curricula to verify that the updated desired outcomes have been achieved. Curriculum designers should also create an implementation plan that supports successful programmatic execution of the curriculum. The implementation plan should include recommended timelines, resources, professional development, and data collection.

See also Alignment, Curriculum Maps, Grain Size, Learning Progressions, Program vs. Curriculum

Conley, David T. 2011. *Crosswalk Analysis of Deeper Learning Skills to Common Core State Standards*. Educational Policy Improvement Center.

Gross, Karen. 2012. *Crosswalks*. Office of the Under Secretary for the U.S. Department of Education. https://sites.ed.gov/ous/2012/05/crosswalks/

DOI: 10.4324/9780429321283-11

✔️ DO

- Do use crosswalks to assess and demonstrate substantial equivalency.
- Do use crosswalks to identify gaps or incongruities between two curricula.
- Do use crosswalks to inform the strategic roadmap for iterating a curriculum.
- Do use a simple, two-column chart when creating a crosswalk.

❌ DON'T

- Don't crowdsource crosswalk creation.
- Don't use the given grain size of the outcomes in two different curricula without adjusting to ensure that they are comparable.
- Don't neglect to maintain, review, and update the crosswalk as the curriculum evolves.

💬 REFLECT

A Curriculum Crosswalk allows for gaps to be found between current coursework and expected knowledge and skills on the job. These gaps and deficiencies can then be used to develop new coursework, new courses, and/or new opportunities for students to gain the necessary knowledge and skills.

Bitters, B., and Wegner, J. 2009. *Crosswalking Curriculum: Incorporating Knowledge and Skill Statements.* Wisconsin Department of Public Instruction. https://dpi.wi.gov/sites/default/files/imce/cte/pdf/curriccrosswalk.pdf

12 Curriculum Assessment

A process or instrument for determining whether and how well the desired results of a curriculum are realized.

The data gathered through assessment are used for many valuable educational purposes. For curriculum design, assessment is the means by which the effectiveness of a curriculum is determined. Assessment data should be used to drive an iterative process through which the curriculum is appraised and continuously improved over time, resulting in an increasingly effective educational program.

The goal of curricular assessment is not to provide feedback to individual students or teachers, but rather to continuously improve a curriculum. To that end, it is necessary to measure whether and how well the desired results of a given curriculum have been achieved. This might include evaluating how the curriculum as a whole delivers on a school's mission, appraising how effectively the enacted curriculum produces the learning outcomes articulated in the intended curriculum, measuring the effectiveness of particular resources, and so on. For example: curriculum designers might analyze items in standardized test results or survey teachers and students for feedback.

Because curricular aims are essentially changes in mindset, behavior, knowledge, and skills, assessments of the curriculum should measure students' growth in order to gauge the curriculum's effectiveness. In turn, assessment methods should be selected based on what is being measured and data must be considered in aggregate: when evaluating the effectiveness of a curriculum, anecdotal evidence is the enemy. Holistic evaluation of standardized test results, project artifacts, written responses, and multiple choice questions is optimal for discovering the effectiveness of the curriculum. While interviews, observations, and surveys are useful tools for evaluating social skills, work habits, and interests, they should not be used to assess a curriculum's effectiveness, though they can be considered in holistic evaluation.

Both the validity and the reliability of curricular assessments must be assured. Validity refers to whether the goals outlined in the intended curriculum have been achieved by the enacted curriculum. Reliability refers to whether those outcomes have been achieved consistently across multiple contexts, such as across different teachers' sections or even in different schools. If an assessment is valid, it answers whether students have learned what was intended. If an assessment is reliable, it answers whether a range of students have learned what was intended. An assessment may be reliable but not valid just as it may be valid but not reliable.

See also alignment, Enacted vs. Intended vs. Assessed, Iteration, Learning Outcomes, Learning Progressions

---

Tyler, Ralph. 1949. *Basic Principles of Curriculum and Instruction*. The University of Chicago Press.

DOI: 10.4324/9780429321283-12

DO ···

- ◆ Do assess the effectiveness of the curriculum and use those data to continuously improve the education program at regular intervals.
- ◆ Do assess how well the curriculum as a whole delivers on the school's mission.
- ◆ Do assess how well the enacted curriculum actually results in the intended learning outcomes.
- ◆ Do assess the effectiveness of particular texts, lessons, activities, and resources.
- ◆ Do holistically assess the effectiveness of curricula using all available evidence, but emphasizing valid and reliable measures of student growth.

 **DON'T** ···

- ◆ Don't use the data derived from an assessment of the curriculum to provide feedback to individual learners or instructors.
- ◆ Don't select assessment methods arbitrarily.
- ◆ Don't solicit feedback on the curriculum at a pace so rapid that it cannot be acted upon and used to improve the curriculum.
- ◆ Don't use anecdotal evidence to evaluate the effectiveness of the curriculum.

 **REFLECT** ···

Neither parents nor the public can be satisfied long with reports about the number of children enrolled and the number of new buildings built and things of that sort. Eventually, parents have a right to know what kind of changes are being brought about in their children . . . We must expect to use evaluation procedures to determine what changes are actually taking place in students and where we are achieving our curriculum objectives and where we must make still further modifications in order to get an effective educational program.

Tyler, Ralph. 1949. *Basic Principles of Curriculum and Instruction*. The University of Chicago Press.

13 Curriculum Maps

A high-level visual tool for documenting milestones in the enacted curriculum over time and ensuring the enacted curriculum satisfies learning outcomes.

Curriculum maps provide a high-level visual overview of how learning outcomes are met through the enacted curriculum. However, a curriculum map is not a mere compliance document: it is a powerful tool that translates learning progressions into an instructional program. To that end, curriculum maps should be used to plan and document the enacted curriculum and to demonstrate how, when, and where learning outcomes are satisfied.

Curriculum maps differ from both lesson plans and scope and sequence documents. Lesson plans are granular descriptions of the activities and resources used in the classroom on a given day. Scope and sequence documents represent the content covered in a given course, tracking what is being taught and when it is being taught. Curriculum maps offer a high-level overview of the instructional program as a whole. They demonstrate the skills and concepts that students learn across a period of time and a wide range of subject areas. The period of time and range of subjects represented on a curriculum map will vary depending on the nature of the instructional program. For example, a curriculum map for fifth grade would likely be scoped to the academic calendar year and would represent core academic courses such as math, science, English, and social studies, whereas a curriculum map for law school might span the three-year arc of the program and range from torts to cyber security law.

A well-designed curriculum map uses the chosen period of time as an organizing device to chunk the skills and concepts taught across subject areas. The resulting product should be a simple visual chart where the columns track the units of study in order and the rows track some combination of outcomes, essential questions, content, skills, and assessments. This format allows viewers to grasp a high-level overview of the whole instructional program in a single eye span. Curriculum mapping is customizable and can be done at the school, division, program, or grade level. As such, the process for curriculum map creation may vary, but it should always be collaborative and iterative.

Curriculum mapping is as much about process as it is about product. A well-designed curriculum map improves instruction by serving many strategic goals, which include but are not limited to: promoting vertical and horizontal alignment, facilitating spiraling, reducing redundancy, preventing gaps, encouraging interdisciplinary connections, aligning assessments across subject areas, and setting expectations among key stakeholders such as families, students, teachers, and school leaders.

See also Alignment, Course Guides, Crosswalks, Learning Outcomes, Learning Progressions

Burns, Rebecca Crawford. 2001. *Curriculum Renewal: Curriculum Mapping.* Vol. 1. ASCD.
Jacobs, Heidi Hayes. 1997. *Mapping the Big Picture. Integrating Curriculum & Assessment K-12.* ASCD.

DOI: 10.4324/9780429321283-13

DO ···

- ◆ Do use curriculum maps to plan and document an instructional program.
- ◆ Do use curriculum maps to demonstrate how, when, and where learning outcomes are met.
- ◆ Do create a simple visual chart that provides a high-level overview of the curriculum in a single eye-span.

DON'T ···

- ◆ Don't mistake lesson plans or scope and sequence documents for curriculum maps.
- ◆ Don't create overly detailed or lengthy documentation for curriculum maps.
- ◆ Don't neglect to maintain, review, and update the curriculum map as the instructional program evolves.

REFLECT ···

Teachers cannot run up and down the halls of their buildings with notepads gathering information about curriculum and assessment. They cannot call every teacher each student has had for the past few years. Constant meetings outside school hours are ineffective and expensive. We need a 21st century approach. Curriculum mapping amplifies the possibilities for long-range planning, short-term preparation, and clear communication.

Jacobs, Heidi Hayes. 1997. *Mapping the Big Picture. Integrating Curriculum & Assessment K-12.* ASCD.

14 Curriculum vs. Program

Curriculum is the what and the why of learning, while program is the when, where, and how.

Program design and curriculum design derive from a common goal: creating effective learning experiences by applying design principles intentionally. Because they share this goal, they are not often distinguished from one another. However, understanding the fine distinctions between curriculum and program enhances the effectiveness of both by enabling them to work together in concert rather than at odds. Curriculum is the what and the why of learning, while program is the when, where, and how.

Because needs, constraints, and resources vary from school to school, a well-designed curriculum is one that can be successfully operationalized in a wide range of conditions. As such, curriculum designers should make programmatic recommendations only when they are based on research. For example: a lab component in science curricula has been shown to increase effectiveness, but requiring a specific kind of lab experience (such as project-based) is unnecessarily prescriptive.

Curriculum designers should articulate learning goals (intended curriculum), inform learning experiences (enacted curriculum), and define what serves as evidence of learning (assessed curriculum) while remaining flexible when it comes to instructional methods, daily schedule, staffing model, and policies. For example: a well-designed unit in which students create a model of a cell to demonstrate their understanding of its parts could be delivered through inquiry-based learning or independent study, three forty-minute classes a week or two sixty-minute sessions, single-discipline instruction or interdisciplinary co-teaching, zero tolerance for missed classes or an allotted number of permissible absences, and so on. Those implementation strategies—which are the domain of program design—should be selected based on what best serves the unique needs of the given school.

While curricula should always be designed backward from the desired results of learning, program design does not often have this luxury. Practical and logistical constraints such as facilities, schedule, staffing, and licensing requirements often have implications for the design of a program. For example: research has shown that adolescents benefit from a later start to the school day, but this may be impossible to implement due to parents' work schedules; similarly, the range of effective pedagogies is limited to direct instruction and small group work if there are forty students in a class. The goal of program design is to create engaging learning environments in which the curriculum can be delivered effectively within the bounds of such constraints.

The best curriculum designs and the best program designs are made to dovetail. Curriculum designers should be aware of the context in which the curriculum will be implemented and program designers should have a deep understanding of the curriculum they will need to schedule, staff, and deliver. Taken together, curriculum plus program equals a whole that is greater than the sum of its parts.

See also Backward Design, Content vs. Skills, Interdisciplinarity, Flexibility Tradeoff, Scalability

Hunkins, Francis P., and Ornstein, Allan C. 2016. *Curriculum: Foundations, Principles, and Issues*. Pearson Education.

DOI: 10.4324/9780429321283-14

✓ DO

- ◆ Do distinguish between curriculum and program to enhance the effectiveness of each one and make them as complementary as possible.
- ◆ Do make research-based programmatic recommendations for the implementation of the curriculum.
- ◆ Do prescribe what the learning goals are, what the learning experience will best deliver on those goals, and what will serve as evidence of learning.

✗ DON'T

- ◆ Don't prescribe rigid or unnecessary implementation strategies for the curriculum.
- ◆ Don't dictate instructional methods, daily schedule, staffing model, and policies.
- ◆ Don't account for facilities, schedule, staffing, and licensing requirements in the design of the curriculum.

❝ REFLECT

Curriculum implementation is much more than handing out new materials and courses of study. For implementation to succeed, those involved must understand the program's purpose, the roles people play within the system, and the types of individuals who are to be affected by interaction with the new curriculum.

Hunkins, Francis P., and Ornstein, Allan C. 2016. *Curriculum: Foundations, Principles, and Issues*. Pearson Education.

15 Development Cycle

Four stages—analysis, design, development, and testing— that characterize an effective creation process for curricula.

The development of a curriculum should progress through four stages, which are sequential in theory but not always in practice: analysis, design, development, and testing. Because the development of a curriculum requires a series of journeys through this cycle, curriculum designers must understand the goals of each stage.

The first stage is analysis, during which the desired elements of a curriculum are identified. This is achieved through conducting market research, soliciting feedback from key stakeholders, understanding accreditation and licensing conditions, and collaborating with subject-matter experts to provide specialized knowledge. For example: market research may reveal a high demand for advanced science electives; parent feedback may indicate a desire for an advisory program; and accreditation may require the inclusion of physical education. Analysis may also be derived from direct knowledge, such as prior school leadership experience or deep familiarity with a competitor school's curriculum.

The second stage is design, during which the data collected from analysis is translated into a set of specifications. The goal at this stage should be to meet requirements in a uniquely mission-aligned way. For example: a progressive school might favor project-based science electives, an advisory program with an emphasis on diversity and inclusion, and an approach to physical education that centers on health and wellness. By articulating the design specifications, curriculum designers name constraints and success criteria explicitly, provide a transparent rationale for decisions, and clarify who must do what in order to develop the curriculum.

The third stage is development, during which the design specifications are translated into an actual curriculum with the help of subject-matter experts who provide case studies, resources, heuristics, best practices, and deep content knowledge. The goal at this stage is to meet the design specifications as precisely as possible. To that end, quality control strategies are essential. Two kinds of processes should be established: processes that reduce variability in the development of the curriculum and processes that ensure specifications are maintained throughout the development cycle. To that end, structured templates, clear guidelines, and regular collaborative workshops should be established to reduce variability and guard against deviation from specifications.

The fourth stage is testing, during which the curriculum is vetted by subject-matter experts and then piloted with small groups of students. Testing ensures that all requirements and design specifications are met, establishes the quality of the curriculum, and provides feedback about how easily, reliably, and faithfully it can be implemented. Discoveries from testing should be incorporated into iterations of the curriculum, which may need to occur in any of the three previous stages. For example: a test might demonstrate that a licensing condition has not been met, or that a design specification has been overlooked, or that there are discrepancies in quality between courses.

See also Backward Design, Iteration, Innovator's Dilemma, Modularity, Templates

Smith, Preston G., and Reinertsen, Donald G. 1998. *Developing Products in Half the Time: New Rules, New Tools.* Van Nostrand Reinhold.
Tyler, Ralph W. 1949. *Basic Principles of Curriculum and Instruction.* University of Chicago Press.

DOI: 10.4324/9780429321283-15

DO ···

- ◆ Do expect to employ the phases of analysis, design, development, and testing multiple times and not always sequentially.
- ◆ Do incorporate discoveries from testing into iterations of the curriculum.
- ◆ Do establish structured templates, clear guidelines, and regular collaborative workshops to reduce variability.
- ◆ Do engage subject-matter experts to support each stage of the development cycle.

 DON'T ···

- ◆ Don't force a linear progression through the development cycle.
- ◆ Don't derive curricular requirements from personal preferences.
- ◆ Don't use an open-ended, unstructured, or variable process for developing the curriculum.

 REFLECT ···

It is often said that curriculum development is a continuous process, rather than a discrete, one-shot affair. Such a statement needs to be taken quite seriously . . . Curriculum design can be, and probably should be, based firmly upon the kind of empirical evidence that can come from successive tryouts and systematic testing.

Gagne, Robert M. 1967. "Curriculum Research and the Promotion of Learning." *Perspectives of Curriculum Evaluation* 1: 19–38.

16 Enacted vs. Intended vs. Assessed

Three major curriculum models used to articulate learning goals, align instruction, assess learning, and drive continuous improvement.

The enacted curriculum is the set of learning experiences with which students engage—or, what is taught. The intended curriculum is the set of learning goals that drive instruction—or, what teachers are expected to enact. The assessed curriculum is the set of learning that is evaluated in order to determine whether (and how well) the enacted curriculum has achieved the learning goals—or, what learning is measured. Understanding how the three work together is essential for a well-designed curriculum that can be continuously improved.

The enacted curriculum is delivered through instruction: for example, a unit of study on the American Civil War or a project in which pi is estimated using experimental methods. Because the enacted curriculum is the most highly visible of the three, many stakeholders—including teachers, administrators, students, families, and the general public—mistakenly assume that the enacted curriculum is the curriculum in total. However, without an intended curriculum that articulates learning goals and an assessed curriculum that measures whether those goals have been achieved, the enacted curriculum is at best arbitrary and at worst purposeless.

The intended curriculum articulates learning goals; famous examples include Common Core, American Council on the Teaching of Foreign Languages, and Next Generation Science Standards. Intended curricula can take many forms including outcomes, progressions, standards, frameworks, pillars, or guidelines. What is included in an intended curriculum varies across countries, states, districts, and schools—and, in some cases, even across programs or divisions within a single school. The degree of flexibility and the extent of sanctions for non-compliance also vary. Regardless of such variances, the intended curriculum should always articulate learning goals such that they could be achieved through different pedagogies and learning tasks. To that end, the intended curriculum is the ends and the enacted curriculum is the means: for example, making a scale model of a cell is one possible means to achieve the end of being able to identify a cell's elements.

Where the intended curriculum is the complete set of learning goals, the assessed curriculum is the subset of learning that is measured—as, for example, on a test. Some have argued that the assessed curriculum should be included in the intended curriculum. But distinguishing the assessed curriculum from the intended is useful because high-stakes tests like the SAT, the Gaokao, or even a driver's test often play an outsized role in determining whether the desired learning has been achieved. Regular comparison between the intended curriculum and the assessed curriculum is good instructional practice and can be quite revealing: a lack of alignment between the two is usually symptomatic of a gap between goals and practice, and thus a sign of a curriculum in need of improvement.

See also Curriculum Assessment, Iteration, Learning Outcomes, Learning Progressions, Program vs. Curriculum

---

Porter, Andrew C., and Smithson, John L. 2001. "Defining, Developing, and Using Curriculum Indicators." *CPRE Research Report Series.*

DOI: 10.4324/9780429321283-16

DO ··

- ◆ Do distinguish between the enacted, intended, and assessed curricula to enhance the effectiveness of each one and make them as complementary as possible.
- ◆ Do define the desired results of learning as a means to anchor enacted learning experiences.
- ◆ Do establish what will be measured in order to determine if the desired results of learning have been achieved.

 DON'T ···

- ◆ Don't design learning tasks or select resources for an enacted curriculum before the intended outcomes have been established.
- ◆ Don't prescribe pedagogies or implementation strategies to achieve the desired results of learning.
- ◆ Don't rely exclusively on high-stakes tests to demonstrate whether or not the desired results of learning have been achieved.

 REFLECT ···

Using a systematic and common language for examining the enacted, assessed, and learned curriculum . . . we were able to demonstrate a strong, positive, and significant correlation (.49) between the content of instruction (that is, the enacted curriculum) and student achievement gains (the learned curriculum).

Porter, Andrew C., and Smithson, John L. (2001). "Defining, Developing, and Using Curriculum Indicators." *CPRE Research Reports*. https://repository.upenn.edu/cpre_researchreports/69

17 Essential Questions

Open-ended, thought-provoking questions that require higher-order thinking and promote transfer.

While inquiry is at the heart of any well-designed curriculum, not all questions are essential questions. An essential question acts as a framing device that situates course content in a broader context, requires higher-order thinking, and focuses learning on transferable ideas. Essential questions are open-ended and do not have a single, definitive, or correct answer; to that end, the rationale for an answer to an essential question is often more important than the answer itself.

Like threshold concepts, the best essential questions promote transfer and call for higher-order thinking skills such as prediction, deduction, inference, analysis, interpretation, and evaluation. Because of this, the grain size of an essential question is often the key to its success. Essential questions should be used for units rather than individual lessons or year-long courses. For example: a unit on chemical reactions might open with an essential question such as "how do substances combine or change to make new substances?" This is a strong unit opener because it sparks further inquiry, but it is too abstract to kick off a single lesson and too narrow for an entire course.

While there are benefits to using essential questions, there are also pitfalls to be avoided. Because essential questions are open-ended by definition, the connection between the essential question and the learning goal that it is meant to situate can easily become murky. For example: if the goal is understanding the causes of World War II, an essential question might be "is war ever justifiable?" Technically, this meets the criteria for an essential question: it is open-ended, thought-provoking, requires higher-order thinking, and promotes transfer. But the question is so philosophical that it is unlikely to yield the desired result of students being able to describe the causes of the second World War. Reframing the question as "was World War II justified?" speaks directly to the goal and orients learners toward what they will be expected to demonstrate in assessments.

Similarly, if essential questions are not anchored in authentic contexts, the benefit of promoting transfer is lost. To use the same example: while debating whether war can ever be justified might make for stimulating classroom conversation, a real-world example (such as World War II) must anchor that debate if it is to be anything more than a thought experiment. If the goal is to promote transfer, the discussion sparked by the essential question should help learners understand the real-world example (such as World War II) and then apply that new understanding to other contexts (such as the Cold War) as well as toward making predictions about the future (such as identifying potential causes of a third World War).

See also Framing, Grain Size, Threshold Concepts

McTighe, Jay, and Wiggins, Grant. 2013. *Essential Questions: Opening Doors to Student Understanding*. ASCD.

DOI: 10.4324/9780429321283-17

✓ DO

- ◆ Do use essential questions to frame a unit of study.
- ◆ Do favor questions that have applicability across multiple content areas.
- ◆ Do facilitate transfer by anchoring essential questions in authentic contexts.
- ◆ Do frame essential questions in ways that promote inquiry.
- ◆ Do use essential questions to focus on the big ideas.

✗ DON'T

- ◆ Don't present learners with essential questions that do not clearly connect to learning goals.
- ◆ Don't frame essential questions in ways that have discrete, close-ended answers.
- ◆ Don't use essential questions for individual lessons or whole courses.
- ◆ Don't feel obligated to craft essential questions for every unit.
- ◆ Don't use essential questions to teach details or minutiae.

🤔 REFLECT

Some teachers frame an essential question that goes off on a tangent. But a good question has to be more than just intriguing. The best essential questions are, literally, of the essence: They take you to the core issues and insights of a topic.

Wiggins, Grant, and Wilbur, Denise. 2015. "How to Make Your Questions Essential." *Educational Leadership* 73 (1): 10–15.

18 Five Hat Racks

Information architecture strategies used to structure a curriculum.

The organization of a curriculum is one of its most powerful features: it is the blueprint of the learner's mental model. It might appear that there are infinite ways to organize a curriculum, but the "five hat racks" principle—named by Richard Wurman and built on the analogy that "hats" are information and "racks" are ways to organize that information—asserts that there are actually only five strategies from which to choose: category, time, location, alphabet, and continuum. These organizational strategies need not be mutually exclusive and can be productively layered to deepen and richen learning experiences.

Category structures the curriculum around relatedness. This strategy is useful when clusters of similarity exist within content. For example: a course on twentieth-century literature using category as its organizing strategy would focus on genre, grouping together works of poetry, fiction, non-fiction, and drama.

Time structures the curriculum around chronological sequence. This strategy is useful when step-by-step procedures are required (such as in a chemistry lab experiment) or when content should be compared over fixed durations. For example: if developing a historical perspective on literature is a learning goal of the twentieth-century literature course, curriculum designers should begin with texts published at the century's start and conclude with texts published at the century's close.

Location structures the curriculum around geographical reference points. This strategy is useful when content is meaningfully related to location. For example, if comparing regional literary styles is a learning goal of the twentieth-century literature course, curriculum designers should group together texts by British authors, Chinese authors, Brazilian authors, Russian authors, and so on.

Alphabet structures the curriculum around alphabetical sequence. This strategy is useful when content is referential, when efficient non-linear access to specific information is required, or when no other organizing strategy is appropriate. For example, while there are few benefits to grouping together authors whose names begin with the same letter in a course, an anthology of twentieth-century literature could use this strategy to great effect.

Continuum structures the curriculum around magnitude. This strategy is useful when content is to be compared across common measures. For example, if fluency in the literary canon is a learning goal of the twentieth-century literature course, curriculum designers should use magnitude of influence as the organizing strategy and group together the most famous texts.

Organizing strategies influence which aspects of the curriculum are emphasized—and, in turn, which aspects are taught and learned. To that end, curriculum designers should first identify the desired learning and then select the organizing strategies that best serve those goals.

See also Advance Organizers, Backward Design, Framing, Mental Models, Storytelling

---

Wurman, Richard Saul. 2000. *Information Design*. MIT Press.

DOI: 10.4324/9780429321283-18

DO ···

- ◆ Do layer different organizational strategies in the curriculum to deepen learning experiences.
- ◆ Do organize information by alphabet when ease of access is paramount or key terms are already familiar.
- ◆ Do organize information by category when clusters of similarity exist within the content.
- ◆ Do organize information by location when geographic comparison or orientation is the priority.
- ◆ Do organize information by time when step-by-step procedures or comparison across temporal periods is the priority.
- ◆ Do organize information by continuum when comparing elements along a common dimension of measure.

DON'T ···

- ◆ Don't select an organizational strategy before identifying the learning goals.
- ◆ Don't use an alphabetical organizational strategy as the default.
- ◆ Don't organize information by category when the relationship between clusters of information is not relevant.
- ◆ Don't organize information by location unless geography is the focus of the curriculum.
- ◆ Don't organize information by time unless a time-based sequence is involved or the learning goal is to compare events over a fixed period of time.
- ◆ Don't organize information by continuum unless comparing elements by magnitude serves the learning goal.

REFLECT ··

While information may be infinite, the ways of structuring it are not. And once you have a place in which the information can be plugged, it becomes much more useful. Your choice will be determined by the story you want to tell.

Wurman, Richard Saul. 1989. *Information Anxiety*. Doubleday.

19 Flexibility Tradeoff

A heuristic for weighing the relative benefits or drawbacks of a curriculum's level of adaptability.

In the context of curriculum design, flexibility means the latitude teachers have in delivering the curriculum. Because teachers and school leaders tend to perceive latitude as desirable, they typically favor flexible curricula. However, flexibility comes with a cost: the quality of alignment to the learning goals will vary far more widely in a flexible curriculum. This can be damaging for learners, especially at scale. It is a common misconception that curricula should be as flexible as possible—in fact, the opposite is usually true.

Providing only a flexible intended curriculum—which outlines learning outcomes without prescribing pedagogies—can pose as many problems as it solves. For example, the Common Core Mathematics Standards detail what students should know or be able to do at the end of the school year, but do not dictate the methods by which those learning goals should be achieved. As such, different students learn the same content (for example, addition and subtraction) in dramatically different ways (problem-based, flipped classroom, lecture, and so on). Inevitably, some of these approaches will be less effective at achieving the learning goal than others. The result is that students' learning experiences are inconsistent across states, districts, schools, and even between two sections within the same grade. Such disparities can create profound—and profoundly disturbing—inequities. By contrast, a more prescriptive curriculum such as Singapore Math delineates tightly sequenced concepts, skills, and methods for achieving learning goals. While Singapore Math is certainly less flexible than Common Core, it has proven more effective at scale: Singapore consistently ranks at the top of international math tests such as the Programme for International Student Assessment (PISA), whereas the United States' math performance is consistently below the international average.

A flexible intended curriculum empowers teachers to exercise creativity in adapting the curriculum and to differentiate instruction, but the success of this approach depends upon teachers' facility in designing learning experiences from scratch. This skill differs from instruction and most teachers need support to develop it. But because professional learning in a flexible curriculum model inherently focuses on outcomes improvement rather than process improvement, training often fails to help teachers develop the skill of learning design. A flexible curriculum may be beneficial in cases where teachers are highly experienced (such as independent schools) or where the goal is to run pedagogical experiments (such as start-up or lab schools). But in most cases, more prescriptive curricula should be favored because they embed learning design and domain expertise, making the curriculum less complex and easier to use. This not only ensures greater consistency and quality in the delivery of the curriculum, but also reduces the burden on teachers, allowing them to provide more targeted coaching to students.

See also Enacted vs. Intended vs. Assessed, Program vs. Curriculum, Scalability

Lidwell, William, Holden, Kritina, and Butler, Jill. 2010. *Universal Principles of Design, Revised and Updated: 125 Ways to Enhance Usability, Influence Perception, Increase Appeal, Make Better Design Decisions, and Teach Through Design*. Rockport.

Short, Jim, and Hirsh, Stephanie. 2020. *The Elements: Transforming Teaching Through Curriculum-Based Professional Learning*. Carnegie Corporation of New York, November.

DOI: 10.4324/9780429321283-19

DO

♦ Do generally favor structured curricula, especially when the priorities are the overall quality, consistency, and scalability of the learning experience.
♦ Do favor a flexible curriculum when teachers are highly experienced or have the bandwidth to iterate curricula regularly.
♦ Do favor a flexible curriculum when the goal is to run pedagogical experiments.
♦ Do make the curriculum more structured with each iteration so as to scale continuous improvement.

DON'T

♦ Don't favor a flexible curriculum when scalability is important.
♦ Don't focus professional development for teachers on outcomes improvement rather than process improvement if using a flexible curriculum.
♦ Don't mistake teachers' domain expertise or instructional skill with an understanding of how to design learning experiences.
♦ Don't favor a structured curriculum in cases where future uses of the curriculum are difficult to anticipate or define.

REFLECT

None of us can manage a device if there are too many choices to be made; we just want to get our jobs done. Moreover, if we give everybody the ability to tailor a product for their own special needs, most people won't bother; it's too complex . . . It's easy to be tempted, but it's not always productive to use the flexibility . . . provide[d].

Norman, Don, and Euchner, Jim. 2016. "Design for Use." *Research-Technology Management* 59 (1): 15–20.

20 Framing

Techniques used to shape how concepts, skills, and information are presented and how learners understand and retain that material.

Framing is the use of images, words, or context to shape how content is understood and remembered. In curriculum design, framing techniques include course titles, essential questions, advance organizers, and so on. Because framing has tremendous influence over which aspects of a given idea are emphasized and recalled, it is frequently used by marketers, propagandists, and others invested in advancing a particular point of view. Curriculum designers can use this technique to their advantage by employing framing to increase students' interest in, engagement with, and retention of concepts and skills.

Using unexpected, surprising, or provocative frames—a common click-bait technique—piques curiosity and generates higher levels of interest. This strategy can be used to promote students' engagement. For example: an art history unit that frames cubism as a revolution in perspective-taking is more likely to capture learners' attention than one that frames cubism as a blurring of linear temporality and a rejection of a singular point of view. While these two descriptions actually say the same thing, the former makes the idea sound exciting and accessible while the latter makes it seem technical and esoteric.

Framing can also be used to emphasize how developing a given skill might serve as either a support or an impediment to students' growth and personal goals. This strategy is most effective when a sense of urgency is created and the short-term benefits of developing the skill are highlighted. For example: to increase interest in a unit on speech-writing, curriculum designers should emphasize how that skill could be used to run for class president or how a well-written speech helps public speakers overcome anxiety when presenting.

In addition to generating interest, framing also increases retention. Concrete, simple frames are more likely to be remembered than longer (even if more accurate) ones. To extend the first example: a unit on cubism titled "Was Cubism Revolutionary?" is more memorable than one titled "Cubism: Non-Linear Temporality and Multiple Points of View in Twentieth Century Art." The first frame uses fun, sticky language. It also employs a question frame that triggers a cognitive response: learners are prompted to formulate an answer.

Negative framing is better remembered than positive. As such, providing examples of what not to do is a more effective strategy than providing examples of something done well. To extend the second example: providing students with a sample of a poorly written or awkwardly delivered speech is more likely to increase their understanding and retention than a sample of a nicely constructed or well-performed one.

See also Advance Organizers, Essential Questions, Five Hat Racks, Labeling Systems, Storytelling, Student-Facing vs. Teacher-Facing

---

Tversky, Amos, and Kahneman, Daniel. 1985. "The Framing of Decisions and the Psychology of Choice." In *Behavioral Decision Making*, 25–41. Springer.

DOI: 10.4324/9780429321283-20

DO ···

- ◆ Do frame topics so as to increase learners' interest in, engagement with, and retention of information.
- ◆ Do favor bold, brief, challenging, and memorable frames.
- ◆ Do favor negative or question frames in cases where retention is important.
- ◆ Do identify how a topic is framed as part of the curriculum design process.

DON'T ···

- ◆ Don't favor accuracy to the detriment of student engagement.
- ◆ Don't use esoteric, lengthy, inaccessible, or complex frames.
- ◆ Don't present multiple conflicting frames for the same topic.

REFLECT ···

This is a question we should be asking ourselves when we think about a problem, a societal problem: How can it be framed? And somebody has the responsibility in those cases of choosing a framing—because it's going to be framed one way or the other. So given that idea that there is no avoiding framing, that you can choose the better frame . . . that's the central idea of behavioral economics and nudging. It's really that: you should choose the frame that leads to the better decision and to the better outcome.

Kahneman, Daniel (#150 The Map of Misunderstanding). "Interview with Sam Harris." *Waking up with Sam Harris.* Podcast Audio. March 12, 2019. www.samharris.org/podcasts/making-sense-episodes/150-map-misunderstanding

21 Grain Size

The level of abstraction at which learning outcomes are articulated.

Learning outcomes can be articulated at different levels of abstraction. For example: "deliver a persuasive argument" and "compose a claim that is contestable, plausible, and provable and support that claim with concrete evidence drawn from reliable sources" describe the same learning goal, but the former paints with a broad brush while the latter has far more texture and detail. This is known as the grain size of the learning outcome. Grain size poses challenges for curriculum designers, who must articulate learning goals for a wide range of skills and knowledge to different stakeholders whose needs are diverse and sometimes mutually exclusive.

The grain size appropriate for one subject area or grade level may be inappropriate for another. For example: literacy is a far broader area of study than organic chemistry and the learning goals for tenth grade mathematics are sure to be more complex than those for first grade. Similarly, the grain size appropriate for one audience may be inappropriate for another. For a teacher, a goal like "deliver a persuasive argument" is too abstract to be useful when creating lessons, developing assignments, or assessing students' work. But the more detailed version of that outcome—"compose a claim that is contestable, plausible, and provable and support that claim with concrete evidence drawn from reliable sources"—would likely be impenetrable and frustrating to parents if it appeared on a report card.

As a general rule, small grain size goals shape instruction and large grain size goals speak to the bigger picture. But goals that are too specific risk missing the forest for the trees just as goals that are too broad risk missing the trees for the forest. For example: while a history teacher might build a unit around key facts and figures of the American Civil War, the larger goal is for students to understand the economic, political, and social conditions that create unrest in a nation-state. At the same time, specific examples (such as slavery, states' rights, Lincoln, and Lee) must first be grasped before students are able to extrapolate broader patterns (such as the causes and consequences of civil conflict). In this way, learning outcomes of smaller grain size serve as training ground for those of larger grain size.

Grain size is ultimately a matter of scale and the key to success is articulating the same learning goal at different levels of abstraction. Accountability for the design of the curriculum as a whole should live at the highest level of abstraction: the school's mission. This ensures that the importance of what students are learning and why they are learning it is immediately evident to all stakeholders.

See also Curriculum Maps, Learning Objectives, Learning Outcomes, Learning Tasks, Propositional Density, Threshold Concepts

---

Ruff, David. 2014. "Thoughts on Grain Size." *Competency Works: Learning From the Cutting Edge*, May 27. https://aurora-institute.org/cw_post/thoughts-on-grain-size/

DOI: 10.4324/9780429321283-21

DO ···

- ◆ Do articulate the same learning goal at different levels of abstraction depending on the audience.
- ◆ Do favor a larger grain size to describe broad topics and big-picture learning goals to non-educator audiences.
- ◆ Do favor a smaller grain size when the goal is to help teachers design or assess learning tasks.
- ◆ Do make parallel units of instruction a parallel grain size.

 DON'T ···

- ◆ Don't select grain size based on personal preference without consideration of the intended audience.
- ◆ Don't use a large grain size for internal-facing documents such as lesson plans or rubrics.
- ◆ Don't use a smaller grain size for external-facing documents such as transcripts or report cards.

 REFLECT ···

If the grain size of test score reports doesn't mesh with the information needs of those who receive those reports, then the reports are almost certain to be of little use. . . . I've heard state department of education officials pat their own backs when telling their state's teachers that every student's score on every single item will be provided. You show me a teacher who wants to go through reports in that tiny, off-putting grain size, and I'll show you a teacher in serious need of a sabbatical.

Popham, James W. 2008. *All about Accountability/Grain Size: The Unresolved Riddle.* ASCD, May 1.

22 Inclusivity

A curricular approach that values, respects, and supports learners, especially when exposing them to challenging ideas or offensive language.

Discussions about inclusivity in education tend to focus on pedagogical practices, but curriculum design is an equally powerful tool for creating inclusive learning environments. To that end, three curricular strategies should be used: inclusive language, support when encountering difficult or upsetting ideas, and opportunities to learn in authentic contexts.

Inclusive language should be integrated into each element of the curriculum design, from ensuring learning goals are accessible to the phrasing of discussion prompts. Consider a learning outcome like "write a contestable claim": if the goal is to demonstrate understanding of what makes a thesis debatable, prescribing a written assessment may pose unintended barriers for students who have physical disabilities, medical diagnoses, or learning differences. To that end, rephrasing that goal as "make a contestable claim" is more inclusive as students would now be able to demonstrate their learning in multiple ways. Similar sensitivity and attention should be paid to the phrasing of discussion prompts. For example, a math problem asking students to calculate an inheritance would likely feel confusing, off-putting, or alienating. Likewise, gender-based pronouns should be avoided throughout the curriculum and replaced with the use of the singular they.

When exposing students to ideas that may be challenging, objectionable, or even offensive, multiple forms of support should be embedded into the design of the curriculum to promote inclusivity. For example: Mark Twain's *The Adventures of Huckleberry Finn* is a classic of American literature, but it is riddled with racial slurs and stereotypes that may upset students. An inclusive curriculum doesn't avoid such difficult elements, but rather acknowledges them at the outset of the unit so that students are prepared for what they will encounter. The unit should include materials that situate the novel in its historical context as well as opportunities for students to conduct their own research on salient contextual topics from slave codes and Jim Crow laws to unreliable narrators and Twain's own political beliefs. Finally, curriculum designers should provide prompts that give students opportunities to reflect upon discomfort, including why they think the text is included in the curriculum and what purpose it serves in their learning. This curricular strategy helps students navigate such challenges, both in texts like *Huck Finn* and in real-world situations they are sure to experience in their own lives.

When it comes to inclusivity, the hands-on work of learning—including the deliverables that students themselves create—is of equal if not greater importance than the language used or the support provided. To that end, opportunities for learning in real-world, authentic contexts should be adopted as much as possible. When student work can be used to make classrooms and communities more inclusive, learners themselves become agents of change who shift the ways in which power structures operate.

See also Case Studies, Framing, Learning Tasks, Mental Models, Storytelling

Banaji, Mahzarin, and Greenwald, Anthony. 2013. *Blindspot: The Hidden Biases of Good People*. Delacorte Press.
Page, Scott E. 2007. *The Difference: How the Power of Diversity Creates Better Groups, Firms, Schools, and Societies*. Princeton University Press.
Steele, Claude. 2011. *Whistling Vivaldi and Other Clues to How Stereotypes Affect Us*. W. W. Norton & Company.

DOI: 10.4324/9780429321283-22

DO ....

- ◆ Do pay close attention to latent assumptions and implicit biases that may permeate the curriculum's language.
- ◆ Do empower students to make their own classrooms and communities more inclusive through hands-on projects.
- ◆ Do promote inclusivity by providing opportunities for students to demonstrate their learning multiple ways.
- ◆ Do equip students to deal with content that challenges their beliefs rather than avoiding that content.

 DON'T ....

- ◆ Don't avoid discomfort or distress when introducing ideas that may be offensive.
- ◆ Don't present challenging or difficult ideas divorced from their historical and cultural context.
- ◆ Don't design assignments that reduce inclusivity to a purely intellectual exercise.

 REFLECT ....

And though no single, one-size-fits-all strategy has evolved, the research offers an expanding set of strategies for doing [inclusivity]: establishing trust through demanding but supportive relationships, fostering hopeful narratives about belonging in the setting, arranging informal cross-group conversations to reveal that one's identity is not the sole cause of one's negative experiences in the setting, representing critical abilities as learnable, and using child-centered teaching techniques.

Steele, Claude. 2011. *Whistling Vivaldi and Other Clues to How Stereotypes Affect Us*. W. W. Norton & Company.

23 Innovator's Dilemma

A model that explains why established, successful curricula still need to be innovated to remain effective in the future.

The innovator's dilemma is a business theory that describes how leading firms can become obsolete even when they are doing everything right. Because these companies provide successful products and services to an established market, they tend to avoid innovative offerings that compete with those products and services. But this actually creates opportunities for start-ups to fill that void, eventually capturing market share and surpassing the established business. The innovator's dilemma provides an urgent cautionary tale for educators: the very things that make a curriculum successful can also render it obsolete.

Established schools—like established companies—have many barriers to innovation, especially when it comes to curriculum. Students and alumni are often sentimentally attached to favorite courses. Faculty are frequently entrenched or even territorial about particular texts, topics, units, and pedagogies. School leaders tend to suffer from sunk-cost fallacy: having invested time and resources into the curriculum (such as teacher training, textbooks, and equipment), they are often loath to make changes. This is all the more the case if the curriculum has proved reasonably effective. Strong leadership and change management are needed to adjust families' expectations about the curriculum being delivered to their children. Finally, systemic arrogance is perhaps the most significant barrier: schools or organizations whose academic reputations are well-established may mistakenly believe that newer or more disruptive curricula are not a threat to them. They do so at their own peril, as evinced by the elimination of SAT II subject tests during the pandemic and the impact of that shift upon the test prep industry's extensive portfolio of curricula.

Curriculum designers seeking to create innovative learning experiences should adopt a few key strategies. Because the effectiveness of a curriculum that does not yet exist cannot be predicted, testing and iteration are essential. To that end, the goal is not to wait until the curriculum is highly polished before piloting it, but rather to do so when it is lean, adaptable, and modular so that it can be iterated quickly and without disrupting the stability of the curriculum design as a whole. Likewise, schools seeking to adopt innovative curricula should run pilots with small cohorts of self-selecting students. This allows the school to experiment with the new curriculum while still maintaining the overall integrity of the academic program.

The innovator's dilemma offers educators a vital lesson: while investing in emerging curricular approaches poses myriad challenges, failing to do so risks obsolescence. Over the last fifty years, nearly every industry has been fundamentally reshaped by a tidal wave of innovation. Education has been spared so far—but the curricular wave is just beginning to crest.

See also Development Cycle, Iteration, Program vs. Curriculum, Scalability

Christensen, Clayton, and Raynor, Michael. 2013. *The Innovator's Solution: Creating and Sustaining Successful Growth*. Harvard Business Review Press.
Christensen, Clayton M. 2013. *The Innovator's Dilemma: When New Technologies Cause Great Firms to Fail*. Harvard Business Review Press.

DOI: 10.4324/9780429321283-23

DO ···

- ◆ Do test new curricula as early as possible.
- ◆ Do share the innovator's dilemma with colleagues—recognition is the first step to solving the dilemma.
- ◆ Do run pilots with small groups of students who have self-selected into the curriculum.
- ◆ Do iterate new curricula quickly.
- ◆ Do favor making your own offerings irrelevant versus waiting for your competition to do so.

DON'T ···

- ◆ Don't assume that established and successful curricula are immune to new and innovative approaches.
- ◆ Don't avoid the opportunity to develop new curricular approaches that might compete with current offerings.
- ◆ Don't slip into the sunk-cost fallacy for curricula.

REFLECT ···

The reason why it is so difficult for existing firms to capitalize on disruptive innovations is that their processes and their business model that make them good at the existing business actually make them bad at competing for the disruption.

Christensen, Clayton M. 2011. "An Interview with Bob Morris." *Blogging on Business*, June 9. https://bobmorris.biz/clayton-b-christensen-a-book-review-by-bob-morris

24 Interdisciplinarity

An approach to curriculum design that deliberately connects ideas and methods from more than one subject area to promote transfer.

The world outside of school is interdisciplinary, but most curricula divide knowledge and skills into discrete subject areas and present them to students as if they bore little relation to one another. By contrast, interdisciplinary learning experiences encourage students to make connections between seemingly disparate ideas and across varying contexts. This can be a powerful curricular technique that encourages transfer, but it is also a double-edged sword to be wielded with care. Curriculum designers should avoid pastiche and favor polymathy in order to put interdisciplinarity to effective use in promoting transfer.

Many so-called interdisciplinary units are merely a hodgepodge of loosely con-nected knowledge and skills drawn from a range of academic disciplines. For example: an interdisciplinary elementary school unit on apples might have students building a model of an apple tree, creating a collage out of crab-apple leaves, visiting an orchard, scaling up an applesauce recipe, and hosting an apple-based food festival to feed the community. This pastiche approach is interdisciplinary for its own sake and is unlikely to promote transfer. While an engaging theme connects multiple subject areas and shapes hands-on activities, it is not clear what the learning goals of this unit are nor how the artifacts that students produce serve as evidence of learning. And without a clear scope and sequence for the content, any transfer is coincidental. By contrast, if the unit had been designed backward from the desired results, the work products would evince the knowledge and skills students had developed. Likewise, if the content had been well-organized around the goal of promoting transfer, the activities would be scoped and sequenced to build background knowledge and create opportunities for students to apply what has been learned in new contexts.

There is a common misconception that interdisciplinary curricula take a generalist approach while subject-specific curricula favor expertise. In fact, the strongest interdis-ciplinary curricula are polymathic: they are both broad and deep, enabling students to bridge together insights from different subject areas and combine ideas in new ways. An interdisciplinary course on food might begin with industrial agriculture before intro-ducing sustainable farming practices, or with nutrition before addressing ethical con-cerns about eating meat. This enables students to build background knowledge—one of the largest determiners of how well and how quickly learners understand and internal-ize new information—while simultaneously creating a multitude of connection points.

See also Background Knowledge, Backward Design, Breadth vs. Depth, Capstones, Case Studies, Learning Outcomes, Learning Tasks, Rigor, Specialization

Burnard, Pam, Colucci-Gray, Laura, and Sinha, Pallawi. 2012. "Transdisciplinarity: Letting Arts and Science Teach Together." *Curriculum Perspectives* 41 (1): 113–118.
Jacobs, Heidi Hayes. 1989. *Interdisciplinary Curriculum: Design and Implementation*. ASCD.
Wiggins, Grant, Wiggins, Grant P., and McTighe, Jay. 2005. *Understanding by Design*. ASCD.

DOI: 10.4324/9780429321283-24

✓ DO

- Do encourage learners to make connections across different fields of knowledge and in varying contexts to promote transfer.
- Do be intentional about incorporating interdisciplinary connections in the design of a curriculum.
- Do seek out opportunities to create interdisciplinary connections across courses.
- Do create a scope and sequence for the content to be covered in interdisciplinary units.
- Do use backward design to ensure that interdisciplinary units serve clear learning goals.

✗ DON'T

- Don't sample knowledge and skills drawn from a range of academic disciplines—intentionally design the learning experience to be cohesive.
- Don't rely upon thematic connections to do the work of learning goals in interdisciplinary units.
- Don't create interdisciplinary connection points to the exclusion of opportunities to apply what has been learned in new contexts.

❝ REFLECT

Interdisciplinary curricula allow students to see patterns in chaos, transcend surface details, and see 'the big picture' that so often eludes us as moderns. Discerning patterns across diverse bodies of content can be motivating to students as well as to the adults who teach them.

Grossman, Pam, Wineburg, Sam, and Beers, Scott. 2000. "Introduction: When Theory Meets Practice in the World of School." In *Interdisciplinary Curriculum: Challenges to Implementation*. Teachers College Press.

25 Iteration

A process of revising a curriculum until an essential number of requirements have been satisfied.

Curriculum iteration is the process by which concepts for learning experiences are explored, tested, and refined based on what succeeded (and what did not) in meeting essential requirements. The degree of change depends on the level of the curriculum's maturity. With each iteration, revisions tend to become smaller, fewer, and further between. Curriculum iteration is incremental, uneven, and never finished: the goal is continuous improvement and excellence is only achieved through many iterations.

Iteration occurs throughout the curriculum design process, beginning with research and analysis. Curriculum designers should identify essential requirements and features through a combination of market research, stakeholder input, and licensing conditions and then iterate the curriculum design accordingly. For example: market research may reveal demand for test prep, feedback may indicate interest in robotics courses, and accreditation may require four years of English. The curriculum design must be refined to account for all of the above.

Once essential requirements have been identified, sample modules should be developed and tested. This is called development iteration and it entails regular internal review in the style of a creative writing workshop or an art school critique. Development iteration is conducted for however long it takes until the curriculum is deemed ready to pilot. Because this can be a time-consuming process and curricula are often subject to time constraints (like the start date of the school year), it may be necessary to employ creative project management strategies (such as using a ready-made curriculum rather than developing a custom-made one). This ensures that development iteration is quality-driven rather than time-driven. While it is natural for new elements of the curriculum to accrue during this phase, pruning should be a goal of development iteration. As such, stakeholder input should not be solicited at this stage. Students, teachers, administrators, and families may not grasp the full range of requirements and their suggestions may be insufficiently informed, premature, or result in progressive additions rather than progressive subtractions.

Once the curriculum is deemed ready to pilot, it should be tested with learners to determine whether the desired outcomes have been achieved. At this stage, it is useful to solicit stakeholder input—but asking for feedback that cannot be acted upon alienates stakeholders and wastes time. When feedback is sought, it should be obtained through controlled interactions rather than open-ended solicitations. Testing can also shed light on problems that may be instructional rather than curricular. For example: if two teachers delivering the same unit have very different results, the problem might be the curriculum or the instruction or both. While the solution might require curriculum iteration, this should not be the default assumption. Programmatic adjustments, professional learning, and aligning expectations may be more direct, efficient, and appropriate solutions.

See also Backward Design, Development Cycle, Flexibility Tradeoff, Innovator's Dilemma

---

Petroski, Henry. 1994. *The Evolution of Useful Things*. Vintage Books.

DOI: 10.4324/9780429321283-25

✔ DO

◆ Do explore, test, and refine concepts for the design of a curriculum.
◆ Do establish clear criteria for defining the degree to which requirements must be satisfied in order for the curriculum design to be considered complete.
◆ Do conduct regular, ongoing internal reviews of sample modules until the curriculum is deemed ready to pilot.

✖ DON'T

◆ Don't consider tests that have been deemed successful more valuable than those that have been deemed failures.
◆ Don't solicit stakeholder input prior to addressing known shortcomings in the design.
◆ Don't use an open-ended, unstructured, or variable process for gathering feedback on tests of the curriculum.

❝ REFLECT

Fundamental design assumptions (and understood limitations) do not become obsolete in a system that develops over decades. Indeed, they can be among the most critical pieces of knowledge that the younger engineers can inherit. The lessons of past failures should also be passed on explicitly to the next generation.

Petroski, Henry. 2006. "Five Questions for Dr. Henry Petroski." *Ask OCE* 1 (10), July 20. https://appel.nasa.gov/2010/02/26/ao_1-10_f_interview-html/

26 Labeling Systems

A technique for clearly, consistently, and efficiently summarizing the key structural elements of a curriculum.

Labels should communicate information simply and economically by summarizing large swathes of information with a few well-chosen words. For example: David Christian's "Big History" curriculum is divided into epoch-based "thresholds" including "Big Bang," "Life on Earth," and so on. This helps users identify familiar concepts, educates them about new ones, and establishes a shared nomenclature. The latter is especially important insofar as it builds the brand of the curriculum and the culture of the school that implements it.

Labels that are clear and pithy are likely to inspire confidence and pique curiosity, while labels that are vague or lengthy are likely to create confusion and lose audiences' interest. Good labels are memorable, but puns, portmanteaus, and clever phrases should be used with care; anything that is overly cute not only risks cringe-worthiness, but also comes at the expense of clarity. Given that curricula must be understood and used by students, teachers, administrators, families, accrediting bodies, policy-makers, and governments, labeling systems should use plain language that is accessible to all of these audiences. For example: while teachers are likely to know the meaning of "formative assessment," students trying to understand how their learning will be measured would find a more straightforward label such as "real-time feedback" easier to understand.

Because labels are ultimately systems, parallel construction is key to success. But labeling inconsistencies across divisions or subject areas are common, as are labeling inconsistencies in grain size and comprehensiveness. For example: a curriculum that takes an interdisciplinary approach to K-12 science might refer to scientific inquiry in the lower school, science, technology, engineering, art, and math (STEAM) in the middle school, and integrated science in the upper school, thus obscuring curricular alignment across divisions. The same is true if the upper school offers "integrated science," but "cross-disciplinary humanities." This also applies to grain size and comprehensiveness: if the title of an introductory language course is "Arabic 101," then an introductory American history course should not be called "Understanding the Past, Present, and Future of U.S. History, Politics, and Government."

Because both clarity and parallel construction are essential to a strong labeling system, any deviation from these principles should be deliberate and strategic. For example: if a school's mission has a particular focus on community engagement, it might be advisable to create a specialized labeling system for that curriculum that emphasizes its unique features. This builds the school's culture with internal stakeholders and the school's brand with external stakeholders: it gives students and teachers a unique common language with which to voice their shared experience while simultaneously equipping admissions, marketing, and college counseling teams with a compelling articulation of what differentiates the school's curriculum.

See also Aesthetics, Alignment, Course Guides, Five Hat Racks, Framing, Stakeholder Assets

Christian, David. 2011. *Maps of Time: An Introduction to Big History*. Vol. 2. University of California Press.
Rosenfeld, Louis, and Morville, Peter. 2002. *Information Architecture for the World Wide Web*. O'Reilly Media, Inc.

DOI: 10.4324/9780429321283-26

DO ....

- Do use labeling systems to create a shared language amongst stakeholders.
- Do favor clear, succinct labels that use accessible language.
- Do prioritize consistency in labeling systems across divisions and departments.

DON'T ....

- Don't use complicated, obscure language in labeling systems.
- Don't use different grain sizes for different labels.
- Don't deviate from the labeling system unless there is compelling reason to do so.

REFLECT ....

It's also important to remember that labels . . . are systems in their own right. Some are planned systems, some aren't. A successful system is designed with one or more characteristics that unify its members. In successful labeling systems, one characteristic is typically *consistency*.

Rosenfeld, Louis, and Morville, Peter. 2002. *Information Architecture for the World Wide Web*. O'Reilly Media, Inc.

27 Learning Objectives

Granular articulations of the goal(s) of a given learning task, which are derived from higher-level learning outcomes.

While learning outcomes articulate what students should know or be able to do at a given benchmark, learning objectives describe the aims of a lesson, activity, or assignment. Outcomes are more general than objectives, but the difference between them is more than just grain size. By breaking down abstract learning goals into concrete learning targets, objectives ensure that the enacted curriculum puts the intended curriculum into practice and that learning can be measured.

For example: an outcome like "apply best practices in public speaking" is too broad to be useful to teachers for planning lessons, activities, and assignments. Smaller, more concrete objectives—such as "shape presentations for an intended audience" or "create visual aids"—are more effective for day-to-day instruction because they are more precise and actionable. To accomplish this objective, students might rewrite a single speech for several groups or work with a slide deck template. Because these activities derive from objectives that were themselves derived from the outcome, the likelihood of achieving the big picture goal of "apply best practices in public speaking" is increased.

Learning objectives are guides for creating effective assessments. A broad outcome such as "develop leadership skills" might inspire an activity like having students role-play a conflict scenario. But this activity could serve any number of objectives, such as understanding a problem from multiple points of view or using techniques of diplomacy to resolve conflicts. Without a clear objective, there is no way to assess if the learning task has achieved the desired result: whether students can argue multiple positions on an issue demonstrates little about their ability to use techniques of diplomacy to resolve conflicts, but it does indicate a great deal about whether they can understand a problem from different perspectives. Just as objectives should derive from outcomes, learning tasks should derive from objectives. This ensures that assigned learning tasks are aligned to broader learning goals.

The best learning objectives are clear, precise, and measurable. They define one kind of skill or knowledge and begin with an unambiguous verb that ties the two together. Frameworks like Bloom's taxonomy can serve as useful reference tools for writing learning objectives because they provide categories of knowledge and skills with corresponding action verbs. Bloom's taxonomy was originally presented as a hierarchy and many educators still make the mistake of using it that way. However, research has shown that the levels are not rigid: it is not the case that students must master one kind of knowledge or skill before another. The structure of observed learning outcomes (SOLO) is a more useful reference point for building learning progressions that move from less to more complex understanding.

See also Curriculum Assessment, Essential Questions, Grain Size, Interdisciplinarity, Learning Outcomes, Learning Progressions, Magician's Code

Anderson, Lorin W., and Krathwohl, David R. 2001. *A Taxonomy for Learning, Teaching, and Assessing: A Revision of Bloom's Taxonomy of Educational Objectives*. Longman.
Biggs, John B., and Collis, Kevin F. 2014. *Evaluating the Quality of Learning: The Solo Taxonomy (Structure of the Observed Learning Outcome)*. Academic Press.

DOI: 10.4324/9780429321283-27

✓ DO

- Do use learning objectives to hold the enacted curriculum accountable to the learning outcomes outlined in the intended curriculum.
- Do derive learning objectives from learning outcomes.
- Do ensure that the curriculum is focused on achieving the intended learning objectives.
- Do create concrete, actionable, and measurable learning objectives to help teachers develop lessons and design assignments that will serve as evidence of learning.

✗ DON'T

- Don't design learning tasks before defining learning objectives.
- Don't list out topics to be covered in a given lesson in place of articulating learning objectives.
- Don't include more than five learning objectives for a single lesson or assignment.

❝ REFLECT

A well formed instructional objective describes the type of learner behavior which is to be produced by the instructional treatment . . . The reason why so many educators have recently been advocating such goal statements is that the reduced ambiguity of the objectives yields a significant increase in the clarity needed both for (1) deciding on the *worth* of the objective and (2) determining whether the objective has been *achieved*.

Popham, W. James. 1971. *An Evaluation Guidebook. A Set of Practical Guidelines for the Educational Evaluator.* Instructional Objectives Exchange.

28 Learning Outcomes

Succinct statements of what students will know or be able to do at a given point in their learning.

Learning outcomes provide a snapshot of what students should know or be able to do at a given benchmark. Crafting learning outcomes is a time-consuming and often fraught process, but it is well worth it: doing so enables stakeholders to align on what is fundamental to the curriculum and ensures that learning experiences are designed in service of achieving curricular goals.

There is a quantity versus quality debate around learning outcomes. The quantity-driven approach equates volume with rigor, setting more and higher expectations in hopes that students and teachers will rise to meet them. The quality-driven approach declutters the curriculum by zeroing in on threshold concepts. Advocates of quantity-driven approach claim that the quality-driven approach dumbs down a curriculum. Advocates of the quality-driven approach argue that the quantity-driven approach overstuffs the curriculum and pushes unreachable expectations onto lower grade levels. For example: quantity-driven curricula often have atoms studied as early as third grade, even though that is long before children are able to grasp the topic. By contrast, quality-driven curricula focus on ensuring that students achieve basic science literacy in the most appropriate principles. In most cases, a quality-driven curriculum is preferable.

To keep learning outcomes quality-driven, they should be expressed in terms of observable behaviors. Articulating that a U.S. history course will cover the Seven Years' War, the American Revolution, and the creation of the Constitution gives an overview of the content, but indicates nothing about what students will know or be able to do at a given point in their learning. Likewise, delineating activities and assignments—such as a debate or a research paper—confuses the means (learning tasks) with the ends (learning outcomes).

Constraints and rationales should be identified in the selection or creation of a set of quality-driven learning outcomes. Constraints might include state and federal policies, licensing requirements, standardized test readiness, academic calendar, school schedule, physical space, union contracts, faculty preparedness, and so on. Rationales might include mission alignment, decreasing the drop-out rate, qualifying for admission to selective colleges and universities, improving long-term employment prospects, and so on. These are not impediments to crafting quality-driven learning outcomes, but rather opportunities to do so with greater intentionality.

See also Enacted vs. Intended vs. Assessed, Grain Size, Learning Objectives, Learning Progressions, Learning Tasks, Subject-Matter Experts, Specialization

Koppal, Mary, and Caldwell, Ann. 2004. "Meeting the Challenge of Science Literacy: Project 2061 Efforts to Improve Science Education." *Cell Biology Education* 3 (1): 28–30.
Wiliam, Dylan, and Leahy, Siobhán. 2016. *Embedding Formative Assessment*. Hawker Brownlow Education.

DOI: 10.4324/9780429321283-28

✓ DO

- ◆ Do use learning outcomes to establish high-level, big-picture learning goals.
- ◆ Do articulate learning outcomes in terms of what students will know or be able to do.
- ◆ Do ensure that learning outcomes are written in such a way that they can be used in assessment.
- ◆ Do generally favor a quality-driven approach over a quantity-driven approach in developing learning outcomes.

✗ DON'T

- ◆ Don't use inconsistent grain sizes for learning outcomes in corresponding content areas.
- ◆ Don't prescribe assessment tasks or rubrics within learning outcomes.
- ◆ Don't frame learning outcomes in terms of non-observable behaviors (such as "recognize," "be aware of," "appreciate," or "understand").
- ◆ Don't confuse topics to be covered or skills to be developed with learning outcomes.

❝ REFLECT

All aspects of the educational program are really means to accomplish basic educational purposes. Hence, if we are to study an educational program systematically and intelligently we must first be sure as to the educational objectives aimed at.

Tyler, Ralph W. 1949. *Basic Principles of Curriculum and Instruction.* University of Chicago Press.

29 Learning Progressions

Purposeful organization of a curriculum into sequenced benchmarks that represent thresholds of progressive competency.

While learning outcomes describe what students will know or be able to do at a given benchmark, learning progressions situate those benchmarks in context. By linking benchmarked outcomes to one another as pivotal stops along the road to a clear end-goal, learning progressions purposefully sequence essential knowledge and skills and ensure that material is neither inadvertently excluded nor unintentionally repeated. As such, learning progressions result in fewer gaps and fewer redundancies across the curriculum.

While there is no definitively correct way to structure learning progressions, they should always meet two criteria: they should be backward designed from the end-goal and they should center on skills and knowledge that can be developed progressively across the arc of an education program. For example: if one aim of a curriculum is for students to become skilled writers of persuasive arguments, a learning progression might include an outcome in which students craft an argument in support of a given claim. In order to master this skill, students first need to present the reasoning underpinning different and opposing positions. Before they can achieve that, they need foundational understanding of specific vocabulary associated with argumentation. In this way, a learning progression for persuasive argumentation links specific outcomes together into a coherent, progressive sequence that begins with the basics of punctuation and culminates in the dissection of common fallacies. Depending on the particular sequencing of outcomes, learning progressions may be more or less accelerated. For example, in some European and Asian countries, students learn algebra in their middle school years, whereas algebra is more commonly taught in high school in the United States.

Because learning progressions typically map a sequence of learning outcomes in a particular academic subject area, some educators have suggested that they might be better understood as content progressions. The rationale for this argument is that learning progressions are most often written by subject-matter experts who are unlikely to be knowledgeable about the science of learning. As such, they risk overvaluing content and may unintentionally champion less effective pedagogies. However, well-constructed learning progressions achieve both goals: they use discipline-specific knowledge as a vehicle to situate the science of cognition within particular content areas.

See also Alignment, Backward Design, Learning Outcomes, Levels, Rigor, Specialization, Subject-Matter Experts

Kim, Helyn, and Care, Esther. 2018. *Learning Progressions: Pathways for 21st Century Teaching and Learning*. The Brookings Institute, Education Plus Development Blog, March 27.
Tyler, Ralph. 1949. *Basic Principles of Curriculum and Instruction*. The University of Chicago Press.

DOI: 10.4324/9780429321283-29

✅ DO ··

- ◆ Do backward design learning progressions from an end-state learning goal.
- ◆ Do engage both education specialists and subject-matter experts in developing learning progressions.
- ◆ Do facilitate vertical alignment by providing professional development opportunities for teacher collaboration across grade levels.
- ◆ Do craft tools to support the successful implementation of learning progressions.

❌ DON'T ··

- ◆ Don't mistake a sequence of topics to be covered for a well-designed learning progression.
- ◆ Don't neglect to adapt established learning progressions to the relevant context.
- ◆ Don't peg a particular benchmark to a specific grade level.

💬 REFLECT ··

The fact that students happen to learn something in a particular sequence does not mean that the sequence is an appropriate learning progression. After all, the particular learning sequence might just be an accident of the particular way that students had been taught. To be useful as a learning progression, there has to be some underlying rationale that students are likely to follow in using this particular sequence in advancing their work.

Wiliam, Dylan, and Leahy, Siobhán. 2015. *Embedding Formative Assessment*. Learning Science International.

30 Learning Tasks

Activities that require the application and practice of knowledge in order to improve retention, develop accurate conceptual models, and increase automaticity.

While engagement is desirable in learning tasks, it is not an end unto itself. Many hands-on activities are merely enjoyable, relying upon a learning-by-osmosis approach that rewards engagement as opposed to understanding. Instead, learning tasks should challenge students to extract sophisticated ideas and make deep connections. Three types of learning tasks achieve this: tasks that develop students' long-term retention, tasks that help students build rich conceptual models, and tasks that increase students' automaticity.

Learning tasks designed to develop long-term retention should limit new information to five pieces total. Students can only engage with approximately five new pieces of information at a time and encountering new information once is not enough to remember it. Further, repeated exposure is needed to consolidate information into long-term memory. Curriculum designers should aid recall by using organizing frameworks and mnemonic devices and by engaging students in applying and retrieving the new information. For example: a glossary in which learners define new key terms in their own words and provide their own examples to illustrate those key terms helps store information in long-term memory and improve retention.

Students must be able to connect information and skills through conceptual models in order to apply what they have learned in real-world contexts. This can be achieved several ways: by engaging students in a simplified version of a complex task, by providing student work samples (which can be scaffolded by leaving out select steps), by engaging learners in relevant thought experiments, and by varying the task to highlight its relevant contextual features. Some examples of conceptual models include: knowing when to use the quadratic equation, demonstrating how to conduct research for a written product, and understanding what kinds of things float.

Recurring skills become automatic with practice. As such, learning tasks designed to increase automaticity should provide ample opportunity for practice and should favor application and recall. To promote transfer, practice tasks should resemble the target context. For example, automatically adding two numbers lined up on a page does not necessarily transfer to automatically adding two numbers in one's head during a conversation. Because automaticity can require a significant amount of time to achieve, learning tasks should be appropriately scoped. For example, an expert pianist can play a song while maintaining a conversation, but a novice pianist must focus on the sheet music, finger positions, and so on.

See also Advance Organizers, Case Studies, Capstones, Content vs. Skills, Framing, Minimalism, Spiral Curriculum, Student Work Samples, Textbooks, Usability vs. Learnability

Van Merriënboer, Jeroen J. G., and Kirschner, Paul A. 2017. *Ten Steps to Complex Learning: A Systematic Approach to Four-Component Instructional Design*. Routledge.
Wiggins, Grant, and McTighe, Jay. 2005. *Understanding by Design*, 2nd ed. ASCD.

DOI: 10.4324/9780429321283-30

DO ··

- ◆ Do backward design learning tasks from learning objectives.
- ◆ Do limit the amount of new information in a given learning task to five pieces total.
- ◆ Do favor learning tasks that require recall and authentic application.
- ◆ Do utilize extensive practice regimens to develop automaticity.
- ◆ Do utilize student work samples to develop students' rich conceptual understanding.
- ◆ Do limit new information to five pieces and utilize mnemonic devices to aid long-term retention.

 DON'T ··

- ◆ Don't treat engagement as an end unto itself when designing learning tasks.
- ◆ Don't engage learners with new information only once.
- ◆ Don't design learning tasks only around content coverage requirements.

 REFLECT ··

Traditional school tasks are highly constructed, well-structured, well-defined, short, oriented toward the individual, and designed to best fit the content to be taught instead of reality . . . Such tasks, though often seen as highly suitable for acquiring simple skills, are neither representative of the type of problems that students' perceive as relevant nor have they proven to be especially effective for acquiring complex skills and competencies or for achieving transfer of learning.

Van Merriënboer, Jeroen J. G., and Kirschner, Paul A. 2017. *Ten Steps to Complex Learning: A Systematic Approach to Four-Component Instructional Design*. Routledge.

31 Levels

An approach to curriculum design that keys courses to different standards of proficiency or aptitude.

In an effort to optimize student achievement and streamline the delivery of instruction, curricula are sometimes designed using levels to distinguish degrees of proficiency. There are two common forms of leveling strategies in curriculum design: creating a single course that can accommodate a range of proficiency levels or creating multiple courses each of which is pegged to a different level of proficiency or aptitude. As a general rule, the former is preferable.

Well-designed curricula support teachers in adapting learning tasks for a range of abilities. For example, students of all proficiency levels learning a new language would likely need to demonstrate an understanding of how to ask for directions. But the learning task assigned to achieve this goal could take many forms: asking simple navigational questions, describing landmarks along a given route, mapping different paths between two locations, or engaging in a debate about the best mode of transportation. These four tasks could be assigned to different students enrolled in the same course depending on the level of each learner's ability or they could be distributed across four different courses pegged at the novice, intermediate, advanced, and expert levels. The former approach is preferable because it helps high-achieving students solidify the foundations of their understanding while simultaneously challenging lower-achieving students to work at the edge of their abilities. Research on reading levels provides further evidence that trying to precisely match levels to students does not actually aid learning—in fact, the opposite seems to be the case. Engaging students with a range of texts, some of which may be below their proficiency level and some of which may be above it, has been shown to be of the greatest benefit to literacy.

Leveled curricula that assume students will be grouped according to their proficiency or ability level deprive both low- and high-achieving students of valuable learning opportunities. Courses that are framed as lower-level reduce expectations for both students and teachers, resulting in a diminished learning experience for all. Students who are placed in remedial courses often internalize the idea that they have lower levels of ability than their peers; this can create a damaging self-concept that persists for years. Meanwhile, students of higher levels of ability or proficiency miss valuable review and teach-to-learn opportunities that allow them to practice retrieval, increase retention, identify and self-assess gaps in their own understanding, and consolidate their knowledge.

Curriculum designers should favor learning tasks that can be easily adapted for mixed-ability groups. To that end, curricula should be carefully scoped and sequenced in order to ensure that students have the requisite knowledge and skills they need to succeed regardless of their level of proficiency. Differentiated levels should be used sparingly and only when there is a significant difference in proficiency (for example, a difference of one academic year).

See also Curriculum Maps, Learning Outcomes, Learning Progressions, Learning Tasks, Rigor, Spiral Curriculum

Benjamin, Rebekah George. 2012. "Reconstructing Readability: Recent Developments and Recommendations in the Analysis of Text Difficulty." *Educational Psychology Review* 24 (1): 63–88.
Steenbergen-Hu, Saiying, Makel, Matthew C., and Olszewski-Kubilius, Paula. 2016. "What One Hundred Years of Research Says About the Effects of Ability Grouping and Acceleration on K–12 Students' Academic Achievement: Findings of Two Second-Order Meta-Analyses." *Review of Educational Research* 86 (4): 849–899.

DOI: 10.4324/9780429321283-31

DO ···

- ◆ Do design curricula that support teachers in differentiating instruction for learners with a wide range of proficiencies.
- ◆ Do carefully scope and sequence learning tasks so that learners are set up for success regardless of their proficiency level.
- ◆ Do design different levels of curricula only when there is at least a one-year difference in proficiency.

DON'T ···

- ◆ Don't design curricula trying to precisely match levels to learners' presumed proficiency.
- ◆ Don't assume a given proficiency is uniform across a given grade level.
- ◆ Don't label courses as lower-level or remedial.

REFLECT ···

If instructional-level placement works, then one would expect to find greater learning in classrooms with multiple small groups. That hasn't been the case.

Shanahan, T. 2014. "Should We Teach Students at Their Reading Levels." *Reading Today* 32 (2): 14–15.

32 Magician's Code

Tricks of the instructional trade—such as learning goals and rubrics—that should be shared with students only in cases where test performance is paramount.

Magicians take an oath: they pledge never to reveal their secrets to any layperson. The magician's code preserves the thrill of the illusion for the audience, alchemizing their experience into wonder. Educators have no such code when it comes to the magic of learning. Jargon-laden goals and rubrics are routinely put in front of students in the name of clarity, even though this practice often results in confusion, disengagement, anxiety, and high cognitive overhead. Curriculum designers should adopt a version of the magician's code: by using a clever sleight of hand to conceal tricks of the instructional trade, curriculum designers can make learning appear to have happened magically.

Learning goals should be presented as engaging, immersive challenges. Even the most earnest efforts to make learning goals accessible and fun for students (such as "I can" statements) break the spell of the learning experience by revealing the educational sausage-making. Instead, curriculum designers should integrate learning goals into activities so seamlessly as to render them invisible. For example: if students learning a new language are asked to describe their family's history, the task is clear, accessible, and engaging. But if the same group were instead instructed to "use the preterite tense to describe a completed action," they would likely become confused, intimidated, or bored.

Evaluation criteria tend to produce anxiety rather than excitement, especially when they are presented in lengthy or complicated rubrics. Students end up spending as much time, energy, and cognitive resources scrutinizing the outcomes detailed in the rubric as they do engaged in the learning experiences that were designed to achieve those outcomes. To make matters worse, the multi-point scales commonly used in rubrics tend to operate on the mistaken assumption that learning progresses linearly or that an activity can only be done one way. When a learning experience is well-designed, students' work products cannot be created without having met the criteria for success. To extend the example above: the sheer fact of a student's ability to describe their family's history is itself evidence of successful use of the preterite tense.

In quality learning—as in quality magic—the tricks of the trade are invisible. However, there is an important exception to this rule: cases where test performance is paramount. As with magic, dissection of a trick requires an understanding of how the trick is performed. When preparing for high-stakes standardized summative assessments like the SAT, the Gaokao, or even a driver's test, students benefit from explicit articulation of the learning goals and success criteria. Cracking the code in this way enables students to devote their attention to performance improvement more effectively and allows instructors to "teach to the test" with greater efficiency and purpose.

See also Learning Outcomes, Learning Objectives, Learning Tasks, Minimalism, Usability vs. Learnability

Carroll, John M. 1990. *The Nurnberg Funnel*. MIT Press.
Hattie, John. 2012. *Visible Learning for Teachers: Maximizing Impact on Learning*. Routledge.
Wiliam, Dylan, and Leahy, Siobhán. 2016. *Embedding Formative Assessment*. Hawker Brownlow Education.

DOI: 10.4324/9780429321283-32

DO ···

- ◆ Do abide the magician's code in curriculum design.
- ◆ Do incorporate learning goals into activities, tasks, and assignments without listing the learning goals for students.
- ◆ Do articulate success criteria in descriptions of activities rather than in student-facing rubrics.
- ◆ Do present students with a list of learning goals and success criteria only in cases where test performance is important.

 DON'T ··

- ◆ Don't present students with a list of learning goals at the outset of a given activity, task, or assignment.
- ◆ Don't use educational jargon in articulating learning goals or success criteria.
- ◆ Don't inflict multi-point scales in rubrics on learners.

 REFLECT ···

And, for the record, just say no to learning-objective slides at the beginning of the course. If you want to communicate the objectives to the learner, use a challenge, a scenario, or a 'your mission, should you choose to accept it' message. There are a multitude of ways that *aren't* bullet points on a slide to accomplish the goals of focusing the learner's attention and letting them know where they are headed.

Dirksen, Julie. 2015. *Design for How People Learn*. New Riders.

33 Mental Models

Cognitive representations of how things work.

From a cognitive science perspective, the goal of education is to develop accurate and complete mental models. Mental models are internal representations of how the external world works. Because they are derived from observation, interaction, experience, assumption, or belief, mental models are often inaccurate or incomplete. But they can be revised, updated, and expanded through learning experiences that are intentionally designed. Students develop mental models that emulate what is presented to them, which is why curricular architecture carries such weight: it is the blueprint of the learner's mental model.

There are three kinds of cognitive structures that give rise to mental models: comparative thinking structures, symbolic representation structures, and logical reasoning structures. Comparative thinking structures—such as classification, spatial orientation, or metaphor—identify similarities and differences between pieces of information. Symbolic representation structures—such as language, mathematics, or graphics—transform information into coding systems. Logical reasoning structures—such as analysis, synthesis, or evaluation—use abstract thinking strategies to process information.

The most robust mental models combine all three cognitive structures and each structure should be leveraged in the design of a curriculum. For example: an activity that uses an advance organizer to sort a given set of objects multiple ways helps students to discover patterns and develop comparative thinking structures; an assignment that asks students to create an infographic helps them to translate information into visual form and develop symbolic representation structures; and a project that asks students to dissect an argument helps them to think critically and develop logical reasoning structures. A curriculum that leverages all three cognitive structures in this fashion is well-positioned to help students develop accurate and complete mental models that achieve learning goals and promote transfer.

Curricula should provide ample opportunities for students to test, revise, update, and expand their mental models. Case studies and thought experiments are especially useful devices for this. Students should be presented with contexts in which their model is applicable and given the opportunity to practice making choices based on their model. Depending on the cost of failure, these opportunities might include role-playing hypothetical scenarios, immersive simulation games, and hands-on projects with real-world consequences. Any learning experience designed to help learners test their mental models should culminate in reflection on and evaluation of the model's applicability, including its usefulness and its limitations. The goal of this is for students to internalize, update, and continuously improve their mentals models so they can be used to explain new information and predict new interactions.

See also Advance Organizers, Background Knowledge, Case Studies, Five Hat Racks, Learning Tasks

Garner, Betty. 2007. *Getting to Got It*. ASCD.
Halford, Graeme S. 2014. *Children's Understanding: The Development of Mental Models*. Taylor & Francis Group.
Johnson-Laird, Philip. 1983. *Mental Models: Toward a Cognitive Science of Language, Inference, and Consciousness*. Cambridge University Press.

DOI: 10.4324/9780429321283-33

DO ··

- ◆ Do provide ample opportunities for learners to test, revise, update, and continuously improve their mental models.
- ◆ Do favor case studies and thought experiments to help learners develop accurate and complete mental models.
- ◆ Do use curricular architecture as a means to help learners develop accurate and complete mental models.
- ◆ Do design learning experiences so that they culminate in reflection on and evaluation of a mental model's applicability.

 DON'T ··

- ◆ Don't expect learners' mental models to evolve without being regularly. challenged so that learners can see where their mental models fail.
- ◆ Don't build curricula that only leverage one kind of cognitive structure.
- ◆ Don't create learning tasks in which students test their mental models with real-world consequences if the stakes of failure are high.

 REFLECT ···

The psychological core of understanding, I shall assume, consists in your having a 'working model' of the phenomenon in your mind. If you understand inflation, a mathematical proof, the way a computer works, DNA or a divorce, then you have a mental representation that serves as a model of an entity in much the same way as, say, a clock functions as a model of the earth's rotation.

Johnson-Laird, Philip Nicholas. 1986. *Mental Models* (Cognitive Science, No 6). Harvard University Press.

34 Minimalism

An approach to curriculum design that engages students in applied learning using the fewest instructional prompts, materials, and scaffolds possible.

It is a common misconception that providing students with ample resources is the best way to achieve learning goals. But less is usually more and quantity does not equal quality—particularly when the goal is applied learning. A minimalist curriculum supports this by using a few key strategies: adopting an action-oriented approach, pruning extraneous content, enabling error recognition and recovery, and curating resources that encourage application.

An action-oriented approach engages students in applied learning as early in the learning process as possible. For example: consider two versions of a unit in which the learning goal is to build a load-bearing bridge. In one version, students are introduced to architectural structures and important bridges around the world before they apply what they learned by building a bridge themselves. In another version, the unit opens with minimal information about bridges and then engages students in attempting to build one. Only after having gained first-hand experience about what works (and what doesn't) in bridge-building are students introduced to architectural structures and important bridges around the world. In the latter approach, students are engaged in productive struggle before learning about possible solutions. This helps them connect the new information to the goal, reveals where more knowledge is needed, and speaks directly to their own experience.

While it is common practice for curriculum designers to present a broad overview of a topic at the outset of a unit, this is not actually the best way to set learners up for success. Providing only what is needed to achieve the goal immediately at hand is preferable. For example, if the bridge-building unit begins with architectural history and key terms, students are spending valuable time on extraneous topics that distract from their goal: to build a bridge that can support the maximum weight. By contrast, providing resources that are focused on the most relevant knowledge—such as common failure points in bridges—maintains motivation by enabling students to apply their learning immediately.

Because error recognition and recovery are essential to learning, curriculum designers should identify the most common sticking points and supply resources that empower students to detect, diagnose, and resolve them. For example: students often struggle to build a bridge that can bear more than twenty pounds. To provide support, curriculum designers should include tests students might conduct to identify whether the failure was caused by the materials, braces, or foundation, as well as recommended strategies for correcting the error.

Instructional materials should interrupt applied learning only when necessary. Resources should be brief and accessible in any order. To that end, short texts or videos should be favored over longer articles or books and prerequisite knowledge should be limited. Content should support activity, not slow it down.

See also Background Knowledge, Learning Progressions, Learning Tasks, Modularity, Rigor, Usability vs. Learnability

Carroll, John (ed.). 1998. *Minimalism Beyond the Nurnberg Funnel*. MIT Press.

DOI: 10.4324/9780429321283-34

✅ DO

- ◆ Do engage students in applied learning as early as possible.
- ◆ Do provide only the information that is absolutely essential to achieving the learning goal.
- ◆ Do identify common sticking points and blockers and supply on-demand resources that learners can use to resolve them.

❌ DON'T

- ◆ Don't present a broad, irrelevant overview at the outset of a unit or course.
- ◆ Don't include information or resources that are tangential to or digressive from the immediate learning goal.
- ◆ Don't distract learners with lengthy lists of supporting resources.

❝ REFLECT

Minimalist instruction is heavily learner oriented. It takes the need that learners have for meaningful activity and sense making as the primary requirement and resource for designing effective training and information.

Carroll, John (ed.). 1998. *Minimalism Beyond the Nurnberg Funnel*. MIT Press.

35 Modularity

A method of managing curricular complexity by dividing a program of study into self-contained units.

Modules are containers that organize the elements of a curriculum into self-contained units. A modular approach encourages intentionally flexible sequencing, reduces internal complexity, and increases scalability. Examples of modular curricula include task-based approaches to language learning and stackable credentials offered by edtech leaders such as Coursera and Udacity.

It is a common mistake to build modules around content to be covered rather than backward designing from learning outcomes. Starting with content negates one of the major benefits of modularity: a curricular system with the fewest possible dependencies. Dependencies between modules are undesirable because they make flexible sequencing impossible, mid-year entry and exit points impractical, and aligning the curriculum to other curricular systems a challenge at best. To create a modular program of study, curriculum designers should design backward, decomposing a course's overarching goals into smaller, unit-level learning goals that do not overlap, rely upon one another, or assume a particular order of delivery. Each individual module within the system should then also be backward designed such that all content, resources, and assessments directly serve the unit's discrete goals. A disciplined approach to pruning extraneous material is necessary for modular curriculum design: any bloat within a given unit increases the likelihood of inadvertently creating dependencies between modules.

Modules should use a parallel structure with regard to unit length, grain size, amount of work, and labeling systems. By reducing the internal complexity of the curriculum in this fashion, parallel structure minimizes cognitive overhead, keeps the focus on the learning goals, and allows students to internalize the module architecture as a mental model for their learning. Further, a recurring parallel structure for both formative and summative assessments enables teachers to more effectively and efficiently gauge students' progress against learning goals. This simplifies the work of differentiation by making possible a competency-based approach that allows students to work through modules at their own pace.

A modular approach is a reliable way to provide and maintain a high-quality curriculum at scale. The inherent flexibility of a modular curriculum makes it well-suited to a variety of instructional contexts including recent popular approaches such as online, blended, and personalized learning. However, these benefits are not without cost: modular curricula are significantly more complex to create than non-modular learning systems. Because of this complexity, curricula should be iterated incrementally with the goal of becoming more modular over time. Curriculum designers must have deep knowledge of the superset of learning goals in order to decompose the intended curriculum into modules. Those modules, in turn, must operate independent of one another while simultaneously functioning together as a whole that is greater than the sum of its parts.

See also Backward Design, Flexibility Tradeoff, Labeling Systems, Scalability, Usability vs. Learnability

Cornford, Ian R. 1997. "Ensuring Effective Learning from Modular Courses: A Cognitive." *Journal of Vocational Education and Training* 49 (2): 237–251.
Ellis, Rod. 2020. "In Defense of a Modular Curriculum for Tasks." *ELT Journal* 74 (2): 185–194.
Modular Course Design. Wiley Education Services. https://ctl.wiley.com/modular-course-design/

DOI: 10.4324/9780429321283-35

DO ···

- ◆ Do modularize curricula to enhance maintainability and scalability.
- ◆ Do minimize dependencies between instructional modules.
- ◆ Do backward design modules from clear learning goals.
- ◆ Do use a consistent parallel structure for all modules.
- ◆ Do iterate the curriculum with the goal of becoming more modular over time.

DON'T ··

- ◆ Don't build modules around content to be covered.
- ◆ Don't underestimate the complexity of creating a modular curriculum.
- ◆ Don't include resources, activities, or assignments in a given module that are tangential to or digressive from the immediate learning goal.

REFLECT ···

It isn't necessary to take an all-or-nothing approach to a modular design: one can mix and match modules as long as they conform to the system's overall design rules. Thus, a modular design process creates at least as many options as there are modules. In other words, modularity *multiplies* the options inherent in a design.

Baldwin, Carliss Young, and Clark, Kim B. 2000. *Design Rules: The Power of Modularity*. Vol. 1. MIT Press.

36 Propositional Density

The amount of information or meaning conveyed by the elements of a curriculum.

Each element of a curriculum—such as an essential question, a learning task, a case study, a course title, and so on—conveys meaning. But like all forms of communication, those that can say more with less are most effective. Just as metaphors and double-entendres embed multiple interpretations within a single phrase, so do curricular components that are rich in meaning embed multiple ideas within a single element. These elements have high propositional density. Incorporating curricular elements with high propositional density (such as threshold concepts) makes the design of the curriculum more compelling, engaging, and memorable.

There are two types of curricular propositions: surface propositions and deep propositions. Surface propositions are simple descriptors that identify conspicuous, perceptible elements. For example, a unit on cells highlights the differences and similarities between plant, animal, and bacteria cells. Deep propositions describe underlying, hidden meanings of those same elements. For example, the same unit on cells could be made more propositionally dense by focusing on the concept of organism: the relatedness between different levels of part-to-whole relationships such as ants to ant colonies, humans as cells in a society, or all life comprising a superorganism at a planetary level. The greater the number of deep propositions per surface propositions, the greater the propositional density.

In a curriculum that has high propositional density, the whole of the curriculum is greater than the sum of its parts. For example: the first paragraph of an essay making a persuasive argument could be presented as a problem frame rather than an introduction. The phrase itself is propositionally dense, clarifying that the issue being introduced at the onset of the argument is not merely a topic for discussion, but rather a problem that needs solving. Because the problem requires a frame, the sorts of anecdotes, comparisons, and generalizations that might have done the trick in a more generic introduction are insufficient. Rather, the frame must provide a meaningful lens through which the audience can understand the problem, make sense out of the disruption the problem has caused, and evaluate the solution being proposed. By using the propositionally dense problem frame instead of a generic introduction, curriculum designers can conjure four essential parts of persuasive argumentation—context (the state of affairs that gave rise to the problem), destabilizing condition (the problem itself), cost (the stakes of the problem), and claim (the proposed solution to the problem)—without requiring the addition of any new elements to the design of the curriculum.

Propositionally dense concepts deliver tremendous bang for buck on both the design and the enactment of a curriculum. Simple elements that are rich in meaning—like the problem frame—imbue an enacted curriculum with depth and nuance by doing more with less.

See also Background Knowledge, Framing, Grain Size, Learning Tasks, Minimalism, Threshold Concepts

Chomsky, Noam. 2009. "Syntactic Structures." In *Syntactic Structures*. De Gruyter Mouton.
Williams, Joseph M., and Colomb, Gregory G. 2007. *The Craft of Argument*. Longman Publishing Group.

DOI: 10.4324/9780429321283-36

DO ···

- ◆ Do favor deep propositions over surface propositions.
- ◆ Do combine simple elements of the curriculum to increase propositional density.
- ◆ Do make sure that deep propositions are complementary rather than contradictory.
- ◆ Do leverage metaphors and analogies to increase propositional density.
- ◆ Do strive to make every element in a curriculum as propositionally dense as possible.

DON'T ···

- ◆ Don't unbundle propositionally dense concepts or frameworks.
- ◆ Don't oversimplify propositionally dense concepts or frameworks.
- ◆ Don't dilute deep propositions with extraneous material.

REFLECT ···

The basic unit of writing sentences is the proposition, not the word or even a sequence of words. The style of our sentences is determined by the ways in which we combine propositions. The sentence rests upon a number of unstated, unwritten propositions that might have been implied or acknowledged by writing this sentence a number of different ways.

Landon, Brooks. 2008. *Building Great Sentences: Exploring the Writer's Craft*. Teaching Company.

37 Proximity

A technique for placing curricular elements close to one another to increase the perception and recall of their relatedness.

Proximity reinforces the relatedness of a curriculum's elements. When elements of a curriculum are presented close to one another in a sequence—whether at the unit, course, or program level—they will be interpreted as being more related than elements that are further apart. For example: if, in a literature course, a Chekhov play is read immediately after a work by Shakespeare, students will be more likely to compare Shakespeare's work with Chekhov's than with another text that appears either later or earlier in that course or with the work of an author who was covered in another course.

To best leverage the benefits of proximity for indicating relatedness, curriculum designers should first carefully choose the curriculum's organizational strategy and then cluster curricular elements together within that strategy to achieve desired learning outcomes. To continue the example above: it would make good sense to group Chekhov and Shakespeare together if the organizing strategy for the course is genre and the learning goal is to develop an understanding of tragedy. Other texts in the course should then be similarly grouped by genre such that tragic works of fiction and poetry are likewise in close proximity to one another. If, however, the organizational strategy for the curriculum were geographical, grouping Shakespeare and Chekhov together would at best serve to reinforce their differences and at worst indicate they were unrelated. Instead, Shakespeare should be in close proximity to other British writers and Chekhov to other Russian writers to signal geographical relatedness.

The same principle applies to the visual elements of a curriculum. To best leverage proximity spatially, curriculum designers should place elements that relate to one another close to each other, ideally within a single eye span. For example, if a referenced graph appears on a separate page than the text that describes it, learners are significantly less likely to recognize, relate, or remember the key point of the referring text than if the graph and accompanying description are presented together.

While proximity is most readily and easily deployed in a course or unit in a given subject area (as in the example above), curriculum designers can fruitfully leverage proximity to help learners make interdisciplinary connections across subject areas. For example, a history unit on the American Civil War might embed a range of STEAM topics such as the design of weapons used in battle or common injuries of the war and their treatments. Finally, curriculum designers should create opportunities for students to identify and map interdisciplinary connections for themselves. Tools such as Venn diagrams, connection circles, cause and effect diagrams, and Euler circles enable learners to make proximate curricular elements that might not otherwise be grouped together.

See also Advance Organizers, Backward Design, Five Hat Racks, Framing, Interdisciplinarity, Learning Progressions

---

Wertheimer, Max. 1999. "Laws of Organization in Perceptual Forms." In *A Source Book of Gestalt Psychology* (ed. Willis D. Ellis), 71–88. Routledge.

DOI: 10.4324/9780429321283-37

DO ···

- ◆ Do be intentional about what learners experience closely together in space and time.
- ◆ Do situate curricular elements in proximity to one another to underscore their relatedness.
- ◆ Do use proximity to highlight and reinforce connections.
- ◆ Do craft learning tasks that ask learners to use Venn diagrams, connection circles, cause and effect diagrams, and Euler circles to make different curricular elements proximate themselves.
- ◆ Do insert a break in either time or space between unrelated elements.

 DON'T ···

- ◆ Don't cluster curricular elements before selecting the overall organizational strategy for the curriculum as a whole.
- ◆ Don't present curricular elements as overlapping when they do not actually share common attributes.
- ◆ Don't use legends or keys instead of direct labels when signaling relatedness between curricular elements.

REFLECT ···

A certain region in the field becomes crucial, is focused; but it does not become isolated. A new, deeper structural view of the situation develops, involving changes in functional meaning, the grouping, etc. of the items . . . Two directions are involved: getting a whole consistent picture, and seeing what the structure of the whole requires for the parts.

Wertheimer, Max. 1945. *Productive Thinking*. Harper & Row Publishers.

38 Rigor

Productively difficult learning experiences that push students to the edge of their abilities.

A rigorous curriculum pushes students to the edge of their abilities while ensuring their social, emotional, and psychological well-being. Difficulty is a required condition for rigor, but suffering is not. To that end, rigor requires setting high standards at the level of the intended curriculum while simultaneously accommodating differentiation at the level of the enacted curriculum. This approach appropriately challenges individual learners whose abilities can—and inevitably will—vary, sometimes quite significantly.

Productive rigor is determined by three key factors: achieving ambitious desired outcomes, students' ability to apply their learning in new contexts, and balancing the edge of students' abilities with their well-being. The level of rigor should also be tied to the stakes of the desired outcomes. For example: a highly demanding curriculum is inappropriate for a preschool, but is entirely appropriate for medical school or combat training.

The most successfully rigorous curricula push students to achieve outcomes under progressively challenging real-world circumstances. Such immersive learning experiences are not hazing rituals nor acts of educational sadism, but rather test kitchens for achieving outcomes under authentic conditions. They also enable students to transfer what has been learned in the classroom to often unpredictable real-world contexts. However, if students' well-being is not ensured, such difficulty can be damaging. Where productive rigor pushes students to the edge of their abilities, unproductive rigor pushes them past that. Unproductive rigor comes at a high cost: learning under stress decreases retention and students bearing the emotional impact of unproductive rigor are more likely to avoid the subject matter or even learn to hate it.

It is worth noting that while curricular difficulty is often lauded, there remains a notable tension between rigor and results: as claims of rigor increase, results often decrease. For example: despite having taken more lab science, algebra, geometry, and English classes than any previous generation (thanks, in large part, to the adoption of state and national standards), American public school graduates are still routinely unprepared for college-level coursework. Content coverage alone does not produce college readiness any more than it constitutes rigor. Rigor is determined not only by what or how much is taught (curriculum), but also by how it is taught (pedagogy) and how it is evaluated (assessment)—which is to say that rigor is ultimately a measure of the learner's holistic experience.

See also Breadth vs. Depth, Content vs. Skills, Enacted vs. Intended vs. Assessed, Usability vs. Learnability

---

Colvin, Richard Lee, and Jacobs, Joanne. 2010. "Rigor: It's All the Rage, But What Does It Mean?" *The Hechinger Report*, April 7.
Soderstrom, Nicholas C., and Bjork, Robert A. 2015. "Learning Versus Performance: An Integrative Review." *Perspectives on Psychological Science* 10 (2): 176–199.

DOI: 10.4324/9780429321283-38

✔ DO

- ◆ Do encourage learners to engage in productive struggle while ensuring their social, emotional, and psychological well-being.
- ◆ Do include case studies, self-assessments, and simulations to increase the rigor of a curriculum.
- ◆ Do set high standards in the intended curriculum that can be differentiated in the enacted curriculum.
- ◆ Do gauge the rigor of a curriculum based on the holistic learner experience and not on the size or difficulty of the curriculum.
- ◆ Do modulate the level of rigor based on age or background knowledge.

❌ DON'T

- ◆ Don't push learners beyond the edge of their abilities.
- ◆ Don't define rigor by the quantity of content in the curriculum.
- ◆ Don't emphasize rigor when the stakes of the desired learning outcomes are relatively low.
- ◆ Don't hold a monolithic definition of rigor—vary it by age, demographic, and so on.

❝ REFLECT

Rigor today should mean more than suffering. As schools courageously embrace a new conception of rigor that rises above merely a crushing workload, we expect to see both increased student wellness and higher levels of more meaningful academic achievement. We owe it to our young people, and to our future, to make this happen.

Jorgenson, Olaf, and Abram, Percy L. 2021. "The Dark Side of Rigor." *Independent School Magazine*, Summer.

39 Scalability

The ability of a curriculum to be effective in as many contexts and for as many learners as possible.

Because creating any complex system from scratch is difficult, the best approach to crafting a scalable curriculum is to start small and simple. This means the curriculum must be adaptable, lean, and modular so that it can be quickly tested and iterated without disrupting the stability of the design. Complexity should only be added once the core aspects of the curriculum have proved effective.

When the goal is to design a curriculum that can scale, the resources, dependencies, and level of expertise required to enact it should be reduced as much as possible without compromising the effectiveness of the curriculum. For example: a STEAM curriculum that assumes access to and use of a 3D printer or a makerspace has very limited scalability and should be iterated with an eye toward making productive use of everyday objects. By reducing both the required resources and the dependencies for implementation, the curriculum is now much easier to scale. Likewise, if the optimal version of this STEAM curriculum requires extensive training for faculty, the level of expertise required to deliver the program successfully should be adjusted. The program should be modified so that the core conditions for curricular effectiveness are met with less required professional development. By reducing the barriers to enactment—such as resources, dependencies, and level of expertise—the scalability of the curriculum is increased.

Because adopters of a curriculum will have a wide range of conditions for success, curriculum designers striving for scalability should minimize contextual and implementation dependencies. Consider the following scenario: a teacher or school leader at a public day school learns about a successful curriculum at a private boarding school and pilots it with their own students. But because that curriculum was tailored specifically for a learning environment in which significant after school study is integral, the public day school pilot does not yield comparable outcomes. The afterschool dependency prevents the curriculum from being scalable to day school contexts since the local school would need to add an afterschool program to achieve comparable outcomes.

Curriculum designers should conduct research and evaluation in order to identify, understand, and enhance the causes of the curriculum's effectiveness and provide appropriate guidance and recommendations to implementation teams. In turn, school implementation teams who have interpreted, adapted, and delivered the curriculum should be regarded as partners whose experiences can be used to improve the impact of the curriculum and increase its scalability.

See also Curriculum vs. Program, Flexibility Tradeoff, Iteration, Innovator's Dilemma, Modularity

---

Coburn, Cynthia E. 2003. "Rethinking Scale: Moving Beyond Numbers to Deep and Lasting Change." *Educational Researcher* 32 (6): 3–12.

Dede, Chris, and Knox, Allyson. 2010. "How to Scale School Success." *Edutopia*, February 17. www.edutopia.org/scale-processes-replication-strategy

DOI: 10.4324/9780429321283-39

✅ DO

- Do favor designs that are adaptable, lean, and modular when the goal is to create a scalable curriculum.
- Do minimize barriers to enacting the curriculum.
- Do minimize the resources, dependencies, and level of expertise required to implement the curriculum successfully when scalability is important.
- Do provide guidance and recommendations about how to implement the curriculum.

❌ DON'T

- Don't assume that an effective curriculum that was designed and developed in one environment will necessarily yield the same results in a different environment.
- Don't require specific implementation strategies such as instructional methods, schedules, or staffing models.
- Don't introduce complexity by designing a highly flexible curriculum when scalability is the goal.

⏲ REFLECT

Be it a medical breakthrough, consumer product, technological innovation, governmental program, or any other enterprise, the path from early promise to widespread impact requires one thing and one thing only: *scalability*—the capacity to grow and expand in a robust and sustainable way. Put simply: you can only change the world at scale.

List, John A. 2022. *The Voltage Effect: How to Make Good Ideas Great and Great Ideas Scale.* Currency.

40 Specialization

Curricula focused on developing a particular skill set or knowledge in a specific area of study.

Valid arguments have been made both for and against specialization. Those in favor suggest that specialized study helps students attain elite levels of proficiency more rapidly. Those against specialized study suggest that intellectual exploration and exposure to a wide range of ideas is an important means to helping students discover their passions organically. Since both arguments have merit, three key factors should be weighed when considering specialization in curriculum design: structure, timing, and level of interest.

Specialized study works best for highly structured domains—such as chess, golf, or coding—where success depends primarily on navigating fixed rules and honing specific skills through experience and practice. When the domains are less structured—which is the vast majority of the time in education—a more generalist approach should be favored. A generalist approach provides a broader contextual knowledge base as well as more opportunities for transfer. Because breadth of experience enables breadth of transfer, curriculum designers should employ the following general rule of thumb: the more structured the application of the learning, the more specialized the curriculum.

Timing is also of the essence when it comes to specialization. Comparisons of specialized study in England (where students apply for a specific field of study while in high school) with Scotland (where students specialize in a specific field only for the second half of their university education) show that earlier specialization resulted in higher starting salaries right out of college. However, the students who specialized early were twenty percent more likely to land in careers not directly related to their college majors within six years of graduation. By contrast, students who specialized later outearned their peers within six years of graduation and were more likely to study fields that directly aligned with their long-term career interests.

Specialization is most effective when there is a high level of interest. To that end, optional electives should be offered to support students with a passion for a given area of study. Contrary to expectation, specialization does not require a uni-disciplinary approach. Interdisciplinary learning can provide opportunities for specialization: for example, a student interested in creative writing might compose a poem about the effects of climate change or the nature of pi. Such interdisciplinary learning experiences provide opportunities to specialize across a variety of contexts, which allows for concentration while still cultivating generalist knowledge and serving students' long-term interests.

See also Breadth vs. Depth, Interdisciplinarity, Learning Outcomes, Rigor

Epstein, David. 2021. *Range: Why Generalists Triumph in A Specialized World*. Penguin.

Ericsson, K. Anders, and Smith, Jacqui (eds.). 1991. *Toward A General Theory of Expertise: Prospects and Limits*. Cambridge University Press.

Malamud, Ofer. 2011. "Discovering One's Talent: Learning from Academic Specialization." *ILR Review* 64 (2): 375–405.

DOI: 10.4324/9780429321283-40

✓ DO

- ◆ Do favor specialized study for structured domains.
- ◆ Do design pathways that allow learners to self-select into specialization at the appropriate time.
- ◆ Do design opportunities for informed exploration prior to specialization.
- ◆ Do create interdisciplinary learning experiences to help students put specialized skills to use across variable contexts.

✗ DON'T

- ◆ Don't design for specialized study when the domain is unstructured.
- ◆ Don't encourage students to specialize before secondary school.
- ◆ Don't promote specialization to the exclusion of generalist knowledge.

❝ REFLECT

When narrow specialization is combined with an unkind domain, the human tendency to rely on experience of familiar patterns can backfire horribly—like the expert firefighters who suddenly make poor choices when faced with a fire in an unfamiliar structure.

Epstein, David. 2021. *Range: Why Generalists Triumph in A Specialized World*. Penguin.

41 Spiral Curriculum

Intentional repetition of key skills and concepts at well-orchestrated intervals throughout a curriculum.

A spiral curriculum introduces and then circles back to essential knowledge and skills at well-chosen intervals. Through this intentional repetition, a spiral curriculum promotes long-term retention, increases accuracy, and facilitates transfer to a wide range of contexts. Curricular spirals can be either short or long and there are benefits to both. However, the contexts in which each is most effective differ as do the strategies required for their implementation.

A short spiral mixes related learning activities in short spans of time—for example, a lesson that includes calculating the area of a circle, a triangle, and an irregular polygon. Short spirals leverage the principle of interleaving, which is the mixing of different types of learning activities to elicit deeper understanding through contrast. This enables students to better distinguish categories and problem types. To that end, short spirals work best when similar problems are mixed—for example, a short spiral that interleaves different kinds of math problems will be much more effective than one that mixes math and literature. High frequency short spirals are optimal: each activity should be practiced a minimum of ten times.

By contrast, a long spiral usually lasts six months or more and has extended periods when the spiraled material is not being learned. For example: a year-long history course in which each unit includes analysis of an important speech is a long spiral. Long spirals leverage the principle of spacing, which breaks practice into small parts with intentional delays in between. This improves students' long-term retention. The frequency and length of the periods of delay is a decisive factor in the effectiveness of a long spiral. In a year-long curriculum, the spiraled activity should occur each month; in a two-year curriculum, it should occur every two months; and so on.

Both short and long spirals enable students to transfer their learning beyond the classroom. Varying the form of spiraled activities highlights their essential characteristics, which allows students to apply their learning more readily in unfamiliar contexts. While varying within a single subject domain is desirable, spiraling across several subject areas multiplies the conceptual connections that students form. For example: studying the use of rhetorical devices in different works of literature is good, but studying the use of rhetorical devices in works of literature and scientific articles is even better. The depth and complexity of the topic should increase with each visit.

See also Alignment, Background Knowledge, Breadth vs, Depth, Interdisciplinarity, Threshold Concepts

Soderstrom, Nicholas C., and Bjork, Robert A. 2015. "Learning Versus Performance: An Integrative Review." *Perspectives on Psychological Science* 10 (2): 176–199.

DOI: 10.4324/9780429321283-41

DO ··

- ◆ Do sprial the design of curricula.
- ◆ Do vary problem types and contexts, introducing them at least ten times for short spirals.
- ◆ Do set review periods at one-tenth the total length of time for longer spirals.
- ◆ Do create opportunities for students to apply their learning on topics or ideas that have already been covered.
- ◆ Do spiral across subject areas.

DON'T ··

- ◆ Don't review material immediately after it has been introduced.
- ◆ Don't use short spirals for activities that are dissimilar.
- ◆ Don't mistake practicing previously learned material with lack of progress.

REFLECT ··

I was struck by the fact that successful efforts to teach highly structured bodies of knowledge like mathematics, physical sciences, and even the field of history often took the form of a metamorphic spiral in which at some simple level a set of ideas or operations were introduced in a rather intuitive way and, once mastered in that spirit, were then revisited and reconstrued in a more formal or operational way, then being connected with other knowledge.

Bruner, Jerome S. 1960. *The Process of Education*. Harvard University Press.

42 Stakeholder Assets

The curricular resources required to meet the wide-ranging needs of a large, diverse group of users.

Curricula have a wide range of stakeholders including teachers, students, school leaders, parents, admissions, marketing, college counseling, and accrediting and licensing bodies. These stakeholders' needs are wide-ranging and sometimes even contradictory, so it is essential to understand how each group will use the curriculum in order to create appropriate resources.

Teachers and students are the most obvious users of the curriculum. Novice teachers should be provided with a combination of learning objectives, units of study, projects, learning tasks, materials, lessons, student work samples, and assessments; experienced teachers generally need fewer materials, but should at minimum be provided with learning goals. Students should be provided with a syllabus or course guide that provides an overview of their program of study, including what will serve as evidence of their learning and what is required to receive credit or graduate.

School leaders must be able to explain the curriculum to diverse stakeholders including faculty, staff, students, families, and external parties. This includes celebrating exemplary instruction and student achievement in school-wide communications, as well as navigating difficult conversations when concerns about the curriculum are raised. In the absence of a thorough understanding of the curriculum, school leaders can create confusion rather than clarity about curricular priorities and goals. To equip school leaders with the necessary depth of knowledge, curriculum designers should provide: learning progressions and a course guide for the programmatic segment that falls under the given leader's purview; a curriculum map that articulates how those learning progressions are enacted; and the rationale behind key curricular choices.

To build and sustain strong stakeholder support, school leaders must be able to offer a compelling narrative about what differentiates their school's curriculum and how it serves their school community. A succinct statement of the philosophy that drives the curriculum is needed, as are illustrative examples of the curriculum in action. These assets should also be suitable for use in marketing, admissions, and college counseling materials including website copy, viewbook content, slide decks, and the school profile required for the college admissions process.

Finally, the curriculum is critical to licensing and accreditation. Licenses are issued by federal, state, or local government bodies, while accreditation is generally a voluntary process of external verification by peer reviewers. Licenses are required for schools to operate; accreditation indicates that a school has met appropriate standards of quality. Because a rigorous audit of the curriculum is common for both licensing and accreditation processes, clear documentation of learning outcomes and progressions are needed, as are accessible curriculum maps and thorough course guides.

See also Alignment, Course Guides, Curriculum Maps, Labeling Systems

Tyler, Ralph W. 1949. *Basic Principles of Curriculum and Instruction*. University of Chicago Press.

DOI: 10.4324/9780429321283-42

✔ DO

- Do provide school leaders with a compelling narrative to understand the curriculum.
- Do identify the different needs of multiple stakeholder groups who interact with the curriculum and tailor assets accordingly.
- Do provide students with clear information about what is required to receive credit or graduate.
- Do equip school leaders with curriculum maps, course guides, learning progressions, and the rationale behind the curricular approach.

✖ DON'T

- Don't assume that an asset that is effective for one audience will necessarily be effective for a different stakeholder group.
- Don't expect administrators, faculty, families, or students to fully comprehend the curriculum design without support.
- Don't provide novice teachers with only a high-level set of learning goals.

❝ REFLECT

If we remember that education is a political activity in which some people influence others, and that the school is one way to organize that power and influence, then perhaps we can try to share the control of the school and use it for our political purposes . . . If we remember this, then we can recognize that the struggle to remake the school is a struggle to make a more just public world.

Huebner, Dwayne. 1975. "Poetry and Power: The Politics of Curricular Development." In *Curriculum Theorizing: The Reconceptualists*, 130–136. McCutchan Publishing Corporation.

43 Storytelling

A method of using narrative devices to make curricula more engaging and memorable.

All good storytelling requires the same five essential elements: setting, characters, mood, plot, and pace. By using these storytelling techniques, curriculum designers can make information more memorable, engaging, and easy to understand.

Setting creates a rich context for what is being learned by providing a sense of time and place. For example, studying pi by learning how Archimedes estimated it in 250 BC in ancient Greece anchors the study of mathematics historically; likewise, learning about Martin Luther King Jr.'s "I Have a Dream" speech in the context of the civil rights movement of the 1960s contextualizes its significance to political activism more broadly.

Characters are the key players who bring the curriculum to life. For example, meeting a working marine biologist or studying Mahatma Gandhi's childhood experiences makes the behavior of whales or the struggle for Indian independence more personal (and thus more memorable). As an additional benefit, research has shown that anchoring ideas in characters helps learners develop empathy.

Mood creates the emotional tone of the curriculum. For example, courses with titles such as "Surviving the Zombie Apocalypse" and "Getting Medieval" feel whimsical and fun; by contrast, if the same two courses were titled "Natural Disasters and Human Behavior" and "Literature of the Middle Ages," a greater sense of rigor and gravitas is conveyed.

Plot provides the curriculum with a clear beginning, middle, and end. At a high level, learning progressions that link outcomes in an intentional sequence provide this kind of structure. At a more granular level, courses, units, and lessons should also have thoughtful plot arcs characterized by clear trajectories. Wherever possible, natural breaks (such as the winter holidays) should be accounted for in the curricular plot just as they would in acts of a play or chapters in a novel.

Pace is the flow of the curriculum. The length of instructional units—whether lessons, units, courses, or even whole programs—should be determined by the difficulty level of the material and the learning outcomes selected. Curriculum designers should recommend appropriate lengths and provide guidance on programmatic chunking strategies.

While additional storytelling elements—such as theme, pattern, conflict, tension, obstacle, or transformation—can be added to further augment the quality of storytelling, none of the five essential elements can be subtracted without detriment. Taken together, the use of storytelling elements in a curriculum engages learners, provides a rich context, evokes an emotional response, and increases the memorability of what has been learned.

See also Five Hat Racks, Framing, Threshold Concepts, Propositional Density

---

Schank, Roger C. 1995. *Tell Me a Story: Narrative and Intelligence*. Northwestern University Press.

DOI: 10.4324/9780429321283-43

DO ··

- ◆ Do use storytelling techniques to provide an engaging context and to make information more memorable.
- ◆ Do use setting to convey a sense of time and place.
- ◆ Do use characters to help learners develop empathy.
- ◆ Do derive the curricular pace from the difficulty of the material and the desired learning outcomes.
- ◆ Do ensure that the curriculum experience has a clear beginning, middle, and end.

 DON'T ···

- ◆ Don't subtract any of the five essential elements of storytelling.
- ◆ Don't create course or unit titles that are incongruous with the mood of the material.
- ◆ Don't craft curricular plots without accounting for natural breaks such as holidays.

 REFLECT ···

Knowledge, then, is experiences and stories, and intelligence is the apt use of experience and the creation and telling of stories. Memory is memory for stories, and the major processes of memory are the creation, storage, and retrieval of stories.

Schank, Roger C. 1995. *Tell Me a Story: Narrative and Intelligence.* Northwestern University Press.

44 Student-Facing vs. Teacher-Facing

Differential design strategies to meet the needs of either students or teachers.

Teachers and students are the two most obvious users of a curriculum. But teachers and students have different needs, and a curriculum that is designed to accommodate both parties rarely succeeds. As such, the design strategy for a teacher-facing curriculum should differ from the design strategy for a student-facing curriculum.

In teacher-facing curricula, the curriculum is written to and for instructors who are able to frame, adapt, or even change the curriculum as they mediate it for students through delivery. Curriculum designers should provide instructors with a clear set of learning goals, a sample scope and sequence, recommended learning activities, resources, assessments, student work samples, and answer keys where appropriate. Experienced teachers will take liberties in adapting the curriculum as they see fit, while novice teachers should be encouraged to stick to the curriculum as written.

In student-facing curricula, the curriculum is written to and for students. Curriculum designers should be highly attuned to elements necessary for students to navigate the learning experience directly including clarity of instructions, deliverables to be submitted, due dates, and reading level (such as sentence length and vocabulary). In a student-facing curriculum, there is often not a teacher to mediate in real time. As such, the quality of both the instructional design and the writing are the keys to success.

For both teacher- and student-facing curricula, understanding how the curriculum is used in practice is essential. Ideally, the curriculum should be tested in advance of publication. But when time and budget constraints preclude this, a process for real-time feedback is necessary so that curriculum designers are well-equipped to respond. However, not all feedback systems are equally effective. Soliciting direct feedback from students and teachers can provide insight on their preferences, but the best methods for gauging the enacted curriculum's effectiveness are students' academic performance and direct observations of the curriculum in action. This is because what best achieves learning goals is often not the same thing as what students or teachers enjoyed most. While it is valuable to understand what made a given unit fun, engagement is a necessary but not a sufficient condition for learning.

See also Curriculum Assessment, Flexibility Trade-Off, Magician's Code

Means, Barbara, Bakia, Marianne, and Murphy, Robert. 2014. *Learning Online: What Research Tells Us about Whether, When and How*. Routledge.

Means, Barbara, Toyama, Yuki, Murphy, Robert, Bakia, Marianne, and Jones, Karla. 2009. "Evaluation of Evidence-Based Practices in Online Learning: A Meta-Analysis and Review of Online Learning Studies." *Director*.

Nielsen, Jakob, and Levy, Jonathan. 1994. "Measuring Usability: Preference Vs. Performance." *Communications of the ACM* 37 (4): 66–75.

DOI: 10.4324/9780429321283-44

✅ DO

- Do establish whether the curriculum is student-facing or teacher-facing and use the appropriate design strategies accordingly.
- Do provide learning goals, scope and sequence, recommended activities, resources, assignments, student work samples, assessments, and answer keys in teacher-facing curricula.
- Do design curricula that can be followed precisely by novice teachers.
- Do design curricula that can be abridged, amended, and extended by experienced teachers.
- Do require publication-grade instructional design and writing for student-facing curricula.
- Do observe the curriculum in action and iterate based on data about students' academic performance.

❌ DON'T

- Don't design curricula that requires experienced teachers to implement the curriculum precisely as it is written.
- Don't rely upon instructor mediation for student-facing curricula.
- Don't prioritize feedback about students' or teachers' personal preferences.

❝ REFLECT

Designing a presentation without an audience in mind is like writing a love letter and addressing it: To Whom It May Concern.

Haemer, Ken, Quoted in Stockil, Tim. 2013. *Start with an Earthquake . . .: How to Make Presentations that Wow Your Audience*. Troubador Publishing Limited.

45   Student Work Samples

Examples of students' work products that make learning outcomes concrete.

The abstract nature of learning outcomes is a blessing and a curse. The blessing is that outcomes generalize across a wide range of contexts and learning experiences. The curse is that outcomes are often so broadly constructed that they lend themselves to multiple interpretations. Student work samples are the common language needed to solve this conundrum because they bring learning outcomes to life.

Student work samples provide concrete, specific examples of what it looks like when a given outcome is achieved. As such, they are powerful tools for helping both teachers and students build accurate and complete mental models of what success looks like for a given learning task. When teachers can compare and analyze sample student work products, their assessments achieve greater reliability and greater consistency than when they use learning outcomes alone. Using student work samples decreases bias in the assessment process, increases curricular alignment, and enables teachers to provide more actionable feedback to students. Sharing student work samples directly with learners encourages detailed, student-led discussions about why and how the sample demonstrates a certain quality of work. And because samples are engaging and memorable, they are more likely to spark students' imaginations, resulting in higher quality learning, increased creativity, stronger retention, and the promotion of transfer. However, caution should be taken to ensure that students' work is non-identifiable so as to keep the focus on the work itself rather than the person who produced it.

The most effective student work samples are not limited to exemplars, but rather include a range of examples at differing levels of quality. Enabling teachers and students to contrast different examples allows them to identify and analyze the characteristics that distinguish high-quality learning task completion, regardless of whether the task is a standardized assessment, a project, a model, a presentation, an essay, or something else entirely. To that end, student work samples that mix the quality levels of superficial and deep features—such as an essay that is well-structured but exhibits poor handwriting or a presentation that is delivered with great confidence but shows only surface-level thinking—are especially thought-provoking challenges. Such examples promote transfer most effectively because they encourage teachers and students to distinguish between characteristics that often coincide with learning and those that clearly demonstrate it.

See also Curriculum Assessment, Enacted vs. Intended vs. Assessed, Learning Outcomes, Magician's Code, Mental Models

Wiliam, Dylan, and Leahy, Siobhán. 2016. *Embedding Formative Assessment.* Hawker Brownlow Education.

DOI: 10.4324/9780429321283-45

DO ··

- ◆ Do provide student work samples to illustrate what the desired results of learning look like with a concrete example.
- ◆ Do share student work samples directly with learners.
- ◆ Do select student work samples that mix quality levels on both superficial and deep features.

DON'T ··

- ◆ Don't include any identifying information in student work samples.
- ◆ Don't only provide examples of excellent work.
- ◆ Don't present student work samples without opportunities for analysis, reflection, and alignment.

REFLECT ···

So, before your students do a laboratory report or write a ghost story, spend some time getting them to look at other students' attempts at similar tasks . . . There are two immediate benefits of getting students to look at samples of student work: first, students are better at spotting mistakes in the work of others than they are in their own work . . . Second, when students notice mistakes in the work of others, they are less likely to make the same mistakes in their own work.

Wiliam, Dylan, and Leahy, Siobhán. 2015. *Embedding Formative Assessment*. Learning Science International.

46 Subject-Matter Experts

Individuals who possess authoritative knowledge in a specific domain and collaborate with curriculum designers to produce effective learning experiences.

Subject-matter experts have deep knowledge or specialized skill in a particular area. Because curriculum designers cannot have content mastery in all topics, subject-matter experts (colloquially known as SMEs) are essential thought partners whose input can provide important guidance that elevates a curriculum and enhances its overall quality. To make the most productive use of partnerships with SMEs, curriculum designers must be skilled at eliciting, leveraging, organizing, and translating SMEs' domain-specific knowledge for learners and utilizing SMEs' expertise to validate the curriculum.

Expert thinking is characterized by a deep understanding, but expertise does not necessarily transfer across domains within a broader area or topic. For example: an expert chess player can easily recall the arrangement of a chess board in mid-play. But if given a chess board with a random arrangement of pieces, the expert player will not recall the arrangement any better than a novice. This has important implications for how subject-matter expertise should be utilized in curriculum design. While a laboratory biologist, a biology curriculum designer, and a biology teacher each have deep knowledge of life sciences, the domains of each of these experts are different enough that transfer is not guaranteed. Each expert's input should be solicited based on their domain-specific knowledge: the laboratory biologist should provide concrete information and ensure technical accuracy; the biology curriculum designer should translate the content provided by the laboratory biologist into a form that is optimal for learners; and the biology teacher should deliver the course to students using effective instructional practices.

Just as curriculum designers may not be SMEs in a given content area, masters of a given content area do not have expertise in curriculum design. Experts tend to take for granted that others share their depth of understanding, explaining concepts at too high a level for a novice to follow. For this reason, SMEs are poor curriculum designers: their expertise is not in maximizing the learnability of content, but rather in the content itself. Curriculum designers should have SMEs render their expertise visually in models and diagrams, draw analogies to common things, think aloud while performing tasks, define terms of art, and provide case studies. It may also be helpful for curriculum designers to use a template that enables SMEs to supply information clearly, succinctly, and effectively. For example: "can you tell me about a typical case?" is a useful question to elicit an overview and "can you give me an example?" or "is X always the case?" are likely to yield the most helpful information on more specific topics. Likewise, "can you render this on a timeline?" or "please show this on a simple flow chart" are likely to reveal relationships and situate information in context.

See also Breadth vs. Depth, Case Studies, Development Cycle, Templates

Frey, Peter W., and Adesman, Peter. 1976. "Recall Memory for Visually Presented Chess Positions." *Memory & Cognition* 4 (5): 541–547.

Hoffman, Robert R., Shadbolt, Nigel R., Burton, A. Mike, and Gary, Klein. 1995. "Eliciting Knowledge from Experts: A Methodological Analysis." *Organizational Behavior and Human Decision Processes* 62 (2): 129–158.

Oakley, Barbara, Sejnowski, Terrence, and McConville, Alistair. 2018. *Learning How to Learn: How to Succeed in School Without Spending All Your Time Studying; A Guide For Kids And Teens.* Penguin.

DOI: 10.4324/9780429321283-46

DO ··

- ◆ Do partner with subject-matter experts to ensure accuracy and authenticity.
- ◆ Do ask subject-matter experts to render their understanding visually, draw analogies, define terms of art, and provide case studies.
- ◆ Do ask subject-matter experts to "think aloud" and explain their reasoning.
- ◆ Do provide subject-matter experts with templates to structure their inputs.

DON'T ··

- ◆ Don't engage subject-matter experts to do the work of instructional design.
- ◆ Don't expect subject-matter expertise to transfer across domains.
- ◆ Don't plug the content supplied by subject-matter experts directly into the curriculum without adaptation.

REFLECT ··

Working with SMEs can be quite challenging . . . At the very beginning, it seems to be a bit awkward . . . It's almost like you were set up on a blind date. And now you're working with this person in order to create a type of a brand new online course, training, or program . . . Whether you're corporate, higher ed, non-profit, whatever entity you're working with—it doesn't matter—all of these things still apply.

Hobson Luke. "How Instructional Designers Build Relationships with SMEs." *The Dr. Luke Hobson Podcast.* Episode 21. https://drlukehobson.com/podcast-episodes/ep-21-how-instructional-designers-build-relationships-with-smes

47 Templates

A tool that increases curricular quality and workflow efficiency by providing a consistent structure for instructional inputs.

Where a curriculum map is a blueprint for the scope and sequence of content in order to ensure that all learning standards are met, a curriculum template performs a more granular function. Templates provide a consistent organizing structure for individual lessons, projects, units, or courses in a program of study. This creates uniformity in the information architecture of the curriculum as a whole, which increases the curriculum's usability and learnability. Templates increase cross-curricular alignment, improve adaptability, encourage iteration, facilitate continuous improvement, promote higher quality outputs, increase workflow efficiency, and embed key design principles that map to students' mental models.

By providing consistent structure, templates reduce cognitive overhead for curriculum designers and allow them to focus their energies on crafting effective, engaging learning activities. While some aspects of a curriculum template should be tailored to the particular needs of the given school or program, there are a few principles that should always characterize a template's design. The first section should be reserved for the learning goals and the second section should be reserved for a brief description of the assessment. By beginning with the end-goal in mind and identifying what will serve as evidence of learning, curriculum designers are better able to internalize backward design, zero in on essential content, prune extraneous content, and produce a lean curriculum that is more likely to achieve its desired results. Whether the curriculum template is intended for building out year-long courses or one-week surveys, time constraints for tasks and activities should be clearly represented. This enables curriculum designers to consider the scope and sequence of what should be learned within the time allotted so that they can chunk content appropriately. A well-designed template should also embed instructions on how to group, order, and prioritize different elements of content.

In general, templates should be designed to be as universalizable as possible. Using a standard template across different subject areas, courses, and projects aligns the curriculum, increases both its usability and its learnability, and helps students build strong mental models. Structural consistency of this kind also enables schools and other learning organizations to produce new or update existing projects, units, and courses more efficiently. Because templates can be easily adapted to meet changing technological, instructional, or course-specific requirements—such as the introduction of a new feature in the learning management system, a shift in the number of instructional weeks in a program, or a laboratory component for a science course—they encourage iteration and continuous improvement of the curriculum. This results in higher overall curricular quality.

See also Backward Design, Flexibility Tradeoff, Learning Outcomes, Scalability, Usability vs. Learnability

Morville, Peter, and Rosenfeld, Louis. 2006. *Information Architecture for the World Wide Web: Designing Large-Scale Web Sites*, 3rd ed. O'Reilly Media.
Wiggins, Grant, and McTighe, Jay. 2005. *Understanding by Design*. ASCD.

DOI: 10.4324/9780429321283-47

✅ DO

- Do use templates to create consistency in the architecture of a curriculum.
- Do reserve the first section of the template for learning goals and the second section for what will serve as evidence of learning.
- Do include sections where the time constraints for tasks and activities are clearly represented.

❌ DON'T

- Don't focus the template exclusively on content to be covered.
- Don't use different templates across different content areas.
- Don't create lengthy or complex templates.

🗨 REFLECT

An instructional planning template can save *intellectual* lives. By having to think of the big ideas; by focusing on transfer as a goal; by worrying about whether goals and assessments align, the Template keeps key design questions front and center that tend to get lost in typical planning, where teachers too easily think about content to be covered instead of minds to be engaged.

Wiggins, Grant. *How Do You Plan? On Templates and Instructional Planning*. https://grantwiggins.wordpress. com/2012/11/30/how-do-you-plan-on-templates-and-instructional-planning/

48 Textbooks

A compilation of content and practice meant to promote learning.

Textbooks are a mainstay of many classrooms, but their effectiveness varies widely. While there is no definitive method for creating effective textbooks, three key factors should be considered: the ability level of the student, the ability level of the teacher, and the set of strategies used to structure the textbook's content.

When students have little background knowledge on a given topic, using a textbook has a much more pronounced effect on their learning. Because textbooks curate the most important concepts and skills and present them in a straightforward manner, they are powerful tools for helping students develop background knowledge. However, as students continue learning and become more advanced in their understanding, using case studies, primary sources, and real-world materials can be equally if not more effective. In fact, at the most advanced levels, a textbook can actually be detrimental to learning—a phenomenon known as the "expertise reversal effect."

Because textbooks curate content, skills, and practice activities, they enable teachers to focus on instruction, feedback, and assessment. Novice teachers in particular benefit from this structure, particularly when clear guidance on how to effectively use the textbook is provided. Curriculum designers can supply this in the form of a teacher's edition. Because experienced teachers are more likely to be able to select or design effective materials and practice activities, strict adherence to a textbook may actually pose unintended barriers to more engaging learning experiences.

Well-designed textbooks generally share a set of structures that work together to promote learning and retention: chunking, practice, information flow, spiraling, and diagrams. Because students can only process a limited amount of information at one time, effective textbooks group together between four and seven new pieces of information. Even better are textbooks that interleave those important chunks of information with practice activities and comprehension questions. Information should flow from the familiar to the unfamiliar. This enables students to develop background knowledge and to situate more abstract content. Additionally, a spiraled approach—which introduces and then circles back to essential knowledge and skills at well-chosen intervals—helps students build connections that support long-term retention. Finally, diagrams and pictures are more likely to be remembered than text alone, particularly when summarizing complex relationships.

In addition to considering students' ability, teachers' ability, and the textbook's structure, curriculum designers must also align the textbook to intended learning outcomes and core pedagogies. However, even a textbook that is aligned to particular standards or instructional methods is not a guarantee of effectiveness. Ultimately, teachers must do the hard work of planning how exactly a textbook will be used in their own courses.

See also Background Knowledge, Content vs. Skills, Interdisciplinarity, Spiral Curriculum, Student-Facing vs. Teacher-Facing

Blazar, David, Heller, Blake, Kane, T., Polikoff, Morgan, Staiger, Douglas, Carrell, Scott, Goldhaber, Dan et al. 2019. *Learning by the Book: Comparing Math Achievement Growth by Textbook in Six Common Core States*. Center for Education Policy Research, Harvard University.

DOI: 10.4324/9780429321283-48

✅ DO

- ◆ Do provide guidance on professional learning that helps teachers use textbooks effectively.
- ◆ Do incorporate clear learning outcomes into the design of textbooks.
- ◆ Do develop practice exercises that match the learning goals of the course.
- ◆ Do include accessible language, spiraling, chunking, pictures, and appropriate information flow in textbooks.

❌ DON'T

- ◆ Don't expect a good textbook to be effective regardless of the teacher.
- ◆ Don't select a textbook based on what other schools or classes do.
- ◆ Don't choose a textbook based on its marketing.
- ◆ Don't limit resource selection to textbooks to the exclusion of other kinds of learning materials.

❝ REFLECT

Textbooks differ in quality and some are much better than others, so not all textbooks will fit this bill. But the likelihood is that you probably recognise most or all of these characteristics in the textbooks you use. Since some approaches work better than others, it is reasonable to consider what we know about effective instruction and about how students learn best in order to improve how textbooks support teaching and learning.

OECD, Singapore. 2010. "Rapid Improvement Followed by Strong Performance." In *Strong Performers and Successful Reformers in Education: Lessons from PISA for the United States.* www.oecd.org/countries/singapore/46581101.pdf

Picardo, Jose. *A Textbook Problem.* www.josepicardo.com/education/a-textbook-problem-seven-suggestions-to-improve-the-quality-of-published-resources/

49   Threshold Concepts
Transformative, paradigm-shifting ideas.

A threshold concept acts as a portal that opens up a new way of thinking about a given topic or discipline. Examples of threshold concepts include the idea of personhood in philosophy, genre in literature, opportunity cost in economics, gravity in physics, and limits in mathematics. Threshold concepts are characterized by a set of distinguishing features: they are transformative, irreversible, and challenging. These features provide a useful heuristic for curriculum designers seeking to distinguish between essential and inessential knowledge and to build curricula focused on durable, transferable skills.

Grasping a threshold concept marks the transformation from thinking like a learner in a given discipline to thinking like an expert in that discipline. For example: a culinary student who comes to understand that the physics of heat transfer are actually a function of temperature gradient would pay newfound attention to whether the pan being used to prepare a particular dish is made of ceramic, cast iron, or stainless steel. To craft learning experiences that enable students to perceive interrelated ideas in the same way that experts in the field would, curriculum designers should partner with subject-matter experts who can provide a deep and integrative understanding of the material.

Once understood, a threshold concept cannot be seen another way. For example: learning about evolution permanently alters students' experience of visiting the primates' habitat at the zoo. Because threshold concepts cannot be unlearned or forgotten, curriculum designers and subject-matter experts may struggle to recall the early stages of their own learning when these concepts still eluded them. To that end, designing such learning experiences requires both empathy and learner research. Further, threshold concepts are relational and many students will need to adopt a recursive approach to learning them. Curriculum designers should favor a spiral approach that revisits the threshold concept in multiple ways and at well-chosen intervals.

Threshold concepts are often difficult to grasp because they challenge tacit, familiar, or common sense understandings of a topic. For example: many students struggle with the idea that a human lifespan is inconsequential in the context of geologic processes. In most cases, the shift produced by grasping a threshold concept is not merely cognitive; it is also affective and might result in exhilaration, frustration, or even distress. To ensure that such struggles are productive for learning, promoting engagement is key. Curriculum designers should provide ample opportunities for learners to explain or represent the threshold concept in their own words, as well as plenty of learning tasks in which students apply or connect the threshold concept to their own experience. Because of their paradigm-shifting nature, threshold concepts should be considered for landmark or capstone learning experiences throughout a curricular arc.

See also Capstones, Inclusivity, Interdisciplinarity, Subject-Matter Experts, Spiral Curriculum

Flanagan, M., Land, R., and Meyer, J. H. F. (eds.). 2016. *Threshold Concepts in Practice*. Sense Publishers.
Land, R., and Meyer, J. H. F. (eds.). 2006. *Overcoming Barriers to Student Understanding: Threshold Concepts and Troublesome Knowledge*. Routledge.

DOI: 10.4324/9780429321283-49

✅ DO ·

- ◆ Do use threshold concepts to benchmark and organize curricula.
- ◆ Do prioritize threshold concepts in the design of activities and assessments.
- ◆ Do identify ideas that meet the criteria for threshold concepts during instructional experiences.

❌ DON'T ·

- ◆ Don't treat threshold concepts as sequential rather than relational.
- ◆ Don't assume that what constitutes a threshold concept in a given curriculum, pedagogy, institution, or nation is universal.
- ◆ Don't dilute threshold concepts with inessential information.

❝ REFLECT ·

A threshold concept can be considered as akin to a portal, opening up a new and previously inaccessible way of thinking about something. It represents a transformed way of understanding, or interpreting, or viewing something without which the learner cannot progress.

Meyer, Jan, and Land, Ray. 2003. *Threshold Concepts and Troublesome Knowledge: Linkages to Ways of Thinking and Practising within the Disciplines*. University of Edinburgh.

50 Usability vs. Learnability

The degree to which a curriculum prioritizes ease of use or effectiveness at achieving learning outcomes.

The human mind has limited attentional and information processing capabilities. When precious cognitive resources are expended on tasks not directly relevant to outcomes, they are wasted. This is compounded by time constraints, which require students to achieve learning goals within a given period of instructional time. For this reason, curricula should challenge learners to think hard about the right things; any extraneous elements should be mitigated or removed. High-quality learning experiences—and the curricula designed to produce them—should be deliberately easy to use and deliberately difficult to learn.

To optimize for usability, curriculum designers should first identify the desired outcomes and then proceed to eliminate any aspects of the learning experience that are not directly germane to those outcomes. When this cannot be achieved, such aspects should be made as deliberately easy as possible. No matter how strong the curriculum design, some cognitive resources will be consumed by administrative overhead—for example, finding the classroom, navigating each teacher's idiosyncratic policies, or learning to use Excel. But these elements can be simplified to minimize the cognitive resources they require. For example, if a curriculum consistently requires submission of a 300-word précis each week, students will increasingly anticipate this assignment; as such, cognitive resources that might have been wasted on navigating expectations are instead dedicated to sustained analysis and composition of the précis. By simplifying extraneous instructions, the curriculum design enables learners to hone in on the most salient aspects of a task with greater ease, to learn new material more quickly, and to engage in productive struggle that speaks directly to learning outcomes.

To optimize for learnability, curriculum designers should strive for engaging content because learning cannot occur without effortful activity on the part of the student. A few key strategies should be used to push students to think about the right things in the right ways: spacing, retrieval practice, and interleaving. Spacing—or, breaking practice into small sessions—promotes retention. While lengthy instructional sessions are often seen as markers of challenging curricula, shorter sessions spaced out over time actually result in better long-term learning. Retrieval practice—or, recalling knowledge to answer specific questions or solve specific problems—increases skill proficiency and long-term retention. By asking students to recall what they have learned, retrieval practice allows learners to identify what they do and do not know and helps teachers differentiate instruction. Interleaving—or, mixing different types of learning activities—facilitates transfer. By presenting a set of related problems for students to solve (for example, volumetric problems mixing cones, spheres, pyramids, and cubes), interleaved curricula ask students to discriminate between different problem types, identify appropriate problem-solving strategies, and apply those strategies in new contexts.

See also Aesthetics, Learning Outcomes, Learning Tasks, Rigor

Krug, Steve. 2000. *Don't Make Me Think!: A Common Sense Approach to Web Usability*. Pearson Education India.
Soderstrom, Nicholas, and Bjork, Robert A. 2015. "Learning Versus Performance: An Integrative Review." *Perspectives on Psychological Science* 10 (2): 176–199.
Willingham, Daniel T. 2021. *Why Don't Students Like School?: A Cognitive Scientist Answers Questions about How the Mind Works and What It Means for the Classroom*. John Wiley & Sons.

DOI: 10.4324/9780429321283-50

✓ DO

- Do make activities related to learning outcomes productively difficult and activities unrelated to learning outcomes as simple as possible.
- Do prune any elements of a curriculum that do not directly serve the learning goals.
- Do simplify any elements of the curriculum that are inessential but cannot be pruned.
- Do increase students' skill proficiency and long-term retention by including ample opportunities for retrieval practice.
- Do mix problem types, problem-solving methods, and learning contexts.

✗ DON'T

- Don't include any extraneous information in the instructions for a given learning task.
- Don't favor lengthy instructional sessions or learning tasks.
- Don't vary learning contexts until students have basic proficiency.
- Don't ask learners to go to multiple websites, keep track of multiple resources, or retain multiple log-ins.

❝ REFLECT

Finally, given that the goal of instruction and practice—whether in the classroom or on the field—should be to facilitate learning, instructors and students need to appreciate the distinction between learning and performance . . . [C]onditions that slow or induce more errors during instruction often lead to better long-term learning outcomes, and thus instructors and students, however disinclined to do so, should consider abandoning the path of least resistance with respect to their own teaching and study strategies.

Soderstrom, Nicholas C., and Bjork, Robert A. 2015. "Learning Versus Performance: An Integrative Review." *Perspectives on Psychological Science* 10 (2): 176–199.

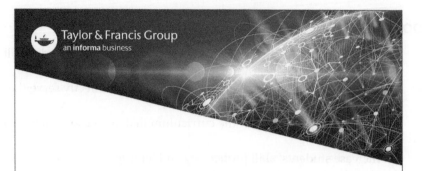